Sects and New Religious Movements

An Anthology of Texts from the Catholic Church
1986-1994

Edited by
The Working Group on
New Religious Movements
VATICAN CITY

Michael-Paul Gallagher, SJ
PONTIFICAL COUNCIL FOR CULTURE
Remi Hoeckman, OP
PONTIFICAL COUNCIL FOR PROMOTING CHRISTIAN UNITY
Ramón Maciás Alatorre
CONGREGATION FOR THE EVANGELIZATION OF PEOPLES
Teresa Osório Gonçalves
PONTIFICAL COUNCIL FOR INTERRELIGIOUS DIALOGUE

To assist those engaged in pastoral ministry and to provide access to documents of the Catholic Church which address sects and new religious movements, the Bishops' Committee for Ecumenical and Interreligious Affairs has recommended publication in English of *Sects and New Religious Movements: An Anthology of Texts from the Catholic Church (1986-1994)*, prepared by the Working Group on New Religious Movements, Vatican City. The English translation of this anthology is authorized for publication by the undersigned.

Monsignor Dennis M. Schnurr
General Secretary
NCCB/USCC

ISBN 1-57455-023-3

TABLE OF CONTENTS

List of Documents

IV EXTRAORDINARY CONSISTORY OF CARDINALS

HOLY SEE

tin, Pontifical Council for Interreligious Dialogue, no. 80, vol. 27 (1992), 209-214. (pp. 25, 45, 52, 59)

33. Poupard, Cardinal Paul, President of the Pontifical Council for Culture. *Felicità e Fede Cristiana,* Piemme, Casale Monferrato, 1992, 115-116. (p. 36)
34. Poupard, Cardinal Paul, "Meno Religiosità e Più Neopaganesimo," in *Jesus,* October 1993, 118-119. (p. 41)

CONTINENTAL SYNODS AND LOCAL CHURCHES

Africa

35. Synod of Bishops: Special Assembly for Africa. *Instrumentum Laboris,* 1993. (pp. 18, 26, 61)
36. Episcopal Conference of Congo. *La Foi Catholique Face aux Nouveaux Mouvements Religieux au Congo: Les Sectes,* April 23, 1988. (pp. 10, 34, 35)
37. Interregional Meeting of Bishops of Southern Africa. *Inculturation: Study Document,* 1993. (pp. 56)
38. Sastre, Robert, Archbishop of Lokossa (Benin). *Réflexions sur les Sectes au Bénin: "Le Christ Est-il Divisé?" (1 Cor 1:13),* 1988. (pp. 23, 33, 35)

Americas

39. IV General Conference of Latin American Bishops. *Conclusions,* 1992, nos. 139-152. (pp. 11, 16, 23, 53, 55)
40. Episcopal Conference of Mexico. *La Iglesia ante los Nuevos Grupos Religiosos,* 1988. (p. 11)
41. National Conference of Catholic Bishops (United States). *Pastoral Statement for Catholics on Biblical Fundamentalism,* March 27, 1987. (pp. 12, 53)
42. National Conference of Catholic Bishops (United States). *National Pastoral Plan for Hispanic Ministry,* 1987. (p. 23)
43. Episcopal Conference of Venezuela. *Instrucción Pastoral sobre el Fenomeno de las Sectas,* 1988. (pp. 11, 25)
44. Bishops of Alabama and Mississippi (United States). *"Toward Your Happiness"—Catholicism and Fundamentalism: A Contrast,* 1989. (pp. 37, 38)
45. Lozano Barragán, Javier, Bishop of Zacatecas (Mexico). "Evangelización y Proselitismo," in *Congreso Iberoamericano sobre "Nueva Evangelización y Ecumenismo,"* October 20-26, 1991. (pp. 24, 32)

59. Raffin, Pierre, Bishop of Metz (France). *Les Sectes ou Nouveaux Mouvements Religieux, Défi Pastoral pour Notre Eglise Diocésaine,* Pastoral Letter, Lent 1992. (pp. 9, 51, 52)

Middle East
60. Gremoli, Giovanni Bernardo, Apostolic Vicar of Arabia. *Pastoral Letter*, January 11, 1987. (p. 22)
61. Sfeir, Cardinal Nasrallah Pierre, Patriarch of Antioch of the Maronites. *L'Eglise et les Sectes*, VI Lenten Pastoral Letter, 1991. (p. 10)

INTRODUCTION

In the encyclical *Redemptoris missio,* Pope John Paul II compared today's society, in which a new search for the spiritual dimension of life expresses itself in many different forms, to an *Areopagus,* similar to that found in Athens by the apostle Paul (cf. Acts 17:22-31). The pope went on to say that people of today also need to be presented with the message of Christ in a new way (cf. *Redemptoris missio,* no. 38).

The contemporary spiritual search often takes the form of "revival" movements within Christianity or within other religions of ancient tradition. But it is also at the basis of many new groups that separate themselves from the mainstream, from institutions, or from doctrines, or that present themselves, in various ways, as radical alternatives for religion or for the dominant culture. The outcome is an increasing fragmentation of the religious world, and this can be seen today on every continent.

From the perspective of the pastors of the Catholic Church, this tendency is a source of worry, insofar as many of the faithful follow doctrines or join groups that distance them gradually from the Gospel and from the Church community. In addition, these groups can sometimes fail to respect the dignity and freedom of the human person. This whole phenomenon has been the reason for many statements by Catholic bishops. Going hand in hand with this pastoral concern is the desire to maintain an attitude of dialogue, in truth and in love, also with those who do not belong to the Church or to the Christian religion.

To cast light on this complex problem of new religious movements and to clarify the attitude of the Church, the Holy See undertook an inquiry with the help of the episcopal conferences, and this led to the preparation of the document *Sects or New Religious Movements: Pastoral Challenge*, published in 1986 by the Secretariats for Christian Unity, for Non-Christians, and for Non-Believers, and by the Pontifical Council for Culture. This text sought to understand the underlying reasons for the phenomenon of the spreading of such groups even within the Catholic community, and it went on to describe the needs and aspirations that these movements seem to answer, all with the aim of reviewing the modes of presence of the Church in the world of today.

A second initiative of the Holy See that gave increased pastoral attention to this area was the extraordinary consistory of cardinals that took place in the Vatican in April 1991. "The Proclamation of Christ, the Only Savior, and the Challenge of the Sects" was one of the two themes of the consistory, chosen by the Holy Father as being especially urgent. The approach taken was basically doctrinal and pastoral.

The Holy Father has frequently voiced his concern about this area and proposed lines of reflection and of response; he has done so through his ordinary catechesis, during his journeys, and in audiences with bishops who come to Rome on *ad limina* visits. Following his example, and seeking to respond to local needs, many episcopal conferences or individual bishops have published, in recent years, pastoral letters or statements, and they have encouraged study of and pastoral initiatives for new religious movements. From the convergence of this documentation one finds "what the Spirit is saying to the churches" (Rev 2:11) in this respect, and, in spite of the diversity of backgrounds, this material can offer light for the entire Christian world.

In order to make the essentials of these pastoral insights available to all it seems opportune to publish this anthology, which is a gathering of quotations from texts of the Holy Father and of the bishops, and occasionally from other documents issued by Church bodies. The necessarily limited selections aim at illustrating the main approaches and principles of discernment proposed by the pastoral documents. Even if the texts are not equally authoritative, as a whole they express the present view of the Church. Except for the bibliography and some other complementary materials, the entire 1986 document is reprinted in the appendix.

The structure chosen to present these short quotations includes, besides a short preface on the universality of the proliferation of the new religious movements, the following chapters:

    I.   Cultural Context and Causes
    II.   Diversity of Origin of the Movements
    III. Impact and Process of Communication
    IV.   Spiritual and Theological Discernment
    V.   Pastoral Challenges and Responses
    VI.   Attitude of Dialogue

The first five chapters offer a brief introduction, an initial section with quotations from the documents of Pope John Paul II, and a second section with quotations from other documents of the Church. After each quotation, the author or place of origin is cited with a number referring to the document listed at the front of this book.

PREAMBLE:
A WORLDWIDE PHENOMENON

Within recent years every continent has witnessed a multiplication of new groups that define themselves as "churches" or "religions" but offer themselves as alternatives to the traditional Christian Churches. They are called, by those who do not belong to them, "sects" or "cults" (terms that generally have a negative connotation) or else "new religious movements (NRMs) or "alternative religious movements."

The final communiqué of the consistory of cardinals of 1991 describes this complex phenomenon, which concerns the Catholic Church insofar as the faithful are not immune to the attractions exerted by such groups:

> This is a changing phenomenon with alarming proportions, and is present almost everywhere, even though with different tendencies and manifestations. In Africa there is the dominant problem of the multiplication of "autonomous churches" that are syncretistic in nature. In Latin America there are communities of an evangelical, fundamentalist, spontaneous nature, which take people away from the unitive Catholic tradition, thus harming the social fabric itself. In the West there are especially groups of a gnostic inspiration. In Asia also the Catholic population of some countries is subjected to an intense sectarian propaganda of independent Christian types.
>
> *IV Extraordinary Consistory of Cardinals, Doc. 24*

In the same consistory, cardinals from different continents described the most striking aspects of this reality in their respective areas:

Africa

> Only at the end of the last century did the sects, religious movements and "independent churches" begin to multiply in the sub-Saharan Africa. . . . Today we must say that it is difficult to determine their number with mathematical certainty, and even more difficult to determine their membership. Every day new sects appear and they in turn give rise to other new movements. Every day members leave one sect to join another.
>
> *Cardinal Alexandre do Nascimento, Doc. 27*

Americas

The Christian sects are the most numerous: the majority are Pentecostals; there are Baptists, Adventists and independent denominations. Almost all these groups call themselves "evangelical churches." The most widespread pseudo-Christian sects are the Jehovah's Witnesses and the Mormons. The sects of Eastern origin are less widespread. . . . There are also societies of a sectarian nature.

Cardinal Ernesto Corripio Ahumada, Doc. 26

It is not easy to describe the religious phenomenon because day by day we speak of "sects" or "cults," whereas many people prefer to call them by the more generic name of "religious movements": Examining this phenomenon in regard to its presence in Latin America, we see them as separatist religious groups or movements that were created in a northern country—the United States—or also, in many cases, at the local level; their characteristics are always their exclusive and exaggerated reliance on the Bible, which is interpreted in a fatalistic sense, and they are generally oriented towards seeking an exclusive society and psychological security through an emotional cult with strong moralistic tones accompanied by anti-Catholic attitudes; they are extremely aggressive and have an immoderate desire for expansion and proselytism.

Cardinal Miguel Obando Bravo, Doc. 28

Asia

. . . emergence and proliferation of fundamentalist and evangelical groups in the Philippines. The need for revitalization became even more acute when these so-called fundamentalist groups began to make inroads even in traditionally Catholic families and institutions, and in the young people. . . .

Cardinal Ricardo J. Vidal, Doc. 31

Europe

We must focus our attention on the phenomenon of the proliferation of the sects and new religious movements. The majority of them originated in the West and come mainly from Christian sectors and Eastern movements; others derive from the occult or the irrational. As a whole, though, they are syncretistic in nature, since they integrate elements of various religions or of other cosmic life principles.

Cardinal Angel Suquía Goicoechea, Doc. 29

1
CULTURAL CONTEXT AND CAUSES

The phenomenon of divisive groups within Christianity is far from new in the history of the Church. Such problems were present even when the New Testament was being written, as many scriptural quotations could illustrate. However, the focus of this anthology is the contemporary pastoral situation.

Concerning the sociocultural background of this phenomenon, most observers believe the extraordinary rate of change in modern times has given rise to impersonal lifestyles and anxieties about meaning and roots. They also emphasize the spiritual situation of culture today. A sometimes desperate search for religious experience is characteristic of so-called "postmodernity," countering the rationalist materialism of earlier modernity.

These cultural contexts differ considerably from continent to continent. In Europe the crisis of industrial and capitalist civilization is highlighted; in Latin America, the situation of poverty and social conflict; in Africa, the crisis of the post-colonial period, the impact of urbanization, and the lack of inculturation by Christianity. In these different settings basic aspirations are evident in different ways: the quest for physical or spiritual healing, for spiritual experience, for the meaning of life, and for relationships with God, with others, and with the cosmos.

DOCUMENTS AND DISCOURSES OF POPE JOHN PAUL II

Cause of NRMs: Secular Culture and the Search for the Spiritual

Our times are both momentous and fascinating. While on the one hand people seem to be pursuing material prosperity and to be sinking ever deeper into consumerism and materialism, on the other hand we are witnessing a desperate search for meaning, the need for an inner life, and a desire to learn new forms and methods of meditation and prayer. Not only in cultures with strong religious elements, but also in secularized societies, the spiritual dimension of life is being sought after as an antidote to dehumanization. This phenomenon—the so-called "religious revival"—is not without ambiguity, but it also represents an opportunity. The Church has an immense spiritual patrimony to offer mankind, a heritage in Christ, who called himself "the way, and the truth, and the life" (Jn 14:6): it is the Christian path to meeting God, to prayer, to asceticism, and to the search for life's meaning. Here too there is an *Areopagus* to be evangelized.

Redemptoris missio, no. 38, Doc. 6

It is not an exaggeration to say that man's relationship to God and the demand for a religious "experience" are the crux of a profound crisis affecting the human spirit. While the secularization of many aspects of life continues, there is a new quest for "spirituality" as evidenced in the appearance of many religious and healing movements that look to respond to the crisis of values in Western society. This stirring of the *homo religiosus* produces some positive and constructive results, such as the search for new meaning in life, a new ecological sensitivity, and the desire to go beyond a cold, rationalistic religiosity. On the other hand, this religious reawakening includes some very ambiguous elements that are incompatible with the Christian faith.

To the Bishops of Iowa, Kansas, Missouri, and
Nebraska (United States), Doc. 13

Cause of NRMs: Weakness in Understanding the Faith

In the extraordinary consistory of the cardinals that I convoked last week, quite a few of the fathers, in analyzing the attraction of the sects, observed that the basis of their spread is often a certain doctrinal confusion about the need for faith in Christ and membership in the Church that he founded. There is a tendency to present religions and the various spiritual expressions pared down to a least common denominator, which renders them practically equivalent, with the result that every person would be free to choose indifferently one of the many ways offered to achieve salvation.

To the Bishops of Abruzzi and Molise (Italy), Doc. 7

Cause of NRMs: Massive Social and Cultural Changes

The other great challenge . . . is the phenomenon of the proliferation and constant expansion of sects, in all of Latin America. . . . Its causes are still in part the object of study and analysis by researchers and experts. One of them is certainly the sociocultural uprooting of great segments of the population: in having migrated from the country to the city, or from one region to another within your immense country, these people are losing the reference points for their religious practice, which many times is tied to places, customs and traditional practices proper to the way in which they have been living.

To the Bishops of the North-2 Region of Brazil, Doc. 4

Cause of NRMs: Fear of Tomorrow

The ideological pluralism, proper to the "secular city," exposes Romans also to a multiplicity of *false offers of salvation*, which creates bewilderment and confusion and throw many people into an attitude of religious indifference. A sign of this is *the proliferation of sects*, which find fertile soil in ignorance and in the fear of tomorrow. . . . Faced with the phenomena of violence and of war and with the occurrence of disasters and misfortunes, one fairly frequently meets people, even those who call themselves Christians, who look for comfort in new religious fellowships or who question the goodness and the fatherhood of God. . . .

Homily During the Visit to a Roman Parish, Doc. 3

Cause of NRMs in Latin America: Strong Economic Support and Preaching That Offers "False Dreams"

I am well aware that the spread of these cults and groups depends on strong economic support and that their preaching tempts people with deceptive illusions, misleads them with distorted simplifications and sows confusion, especially among the simplest and those most lacking in religious instruction.

To the Episcopal Conference of Brazil, Doc. 9

OTHER DOCUMENTS OF THE CHURCH

General Causes of a Psychological and Spiritual Nature

The phenomenon seems to be symptomatic of the *depersonalizing structures* of contemporary society, largely produced in the West and widely exported to the rest of the world, which create multiple crisis situations on the individual as well as on the social level. These crisis situations reveal various needs, aspirations, and questions that, in turn, call for psychological and spiritual responses.

The sects claim to have, and to give, these responses. They do this on both the affective and the cognitive level, often responding to the affective needs in a way that deadens the cognitive faculties.

These basic needs and aspirations can be described as so many expressions of the human search for wholeness and harmony, participation and realization, on all the levels of human existence and experience; as so many attempts to meet the human quest for truth and meaning, for those constitutive values which at certain times in collective as well as individual history seem to be hidden, broken, or lost, especially in the case of people who are upset by rapid change, acute stress, fear, etc.

Secretariat for Promoting Christian Unity,
Secretariat for Non-Christians, Secretariat for Non-Believers,
and Pontifical Council for Culture, Doc. 23

The NRMs indicate that there are spiritual needs that have not been identified, or that the Church and other religious institutions have either not perceived or not succeeded in meeting.

The NRMs can arise or attract because people are searching for meaning when they are feeling lost in a period of cultural change.

Many Christians join the sects or NRMs because they feel that in them there is an answer to their thirst for Scripture reading, singing, dancing, emotional satisfaction, and concrete and clear answers.

There are people . . . who seek in religion an answer to, and a protection against . . . suffering, sickness and death. The NRMs seem to them to confront these existential problems openly and to promise instant remedies, especially physical and psychological healing.

Cardinal Francis Arinze, Doc. 25

Europe: Causes and Context

Among the *psychological* causes we should mention the following: the insecurity, anguish and fear of the people of today, which is caused by the crisis of values and the rapid, profound changes that they are causing in contemporary society, and the tenacious, ruthless struggle for survival. . . . Among the *social* factors that cause or affect this phenomenon we should highlight the family crisis. The emptiness and loneliness caused in members of broken families or those lacking warmth offers these religious groups an extremely receptive medium for their direct and effective work in the field of the family, a field which today has been neglected by some and mistreated by others.

Cardinal Angel Suquía Goicoechea, Doc. 29

If we look closely, we observe that many adepts of "sects" and "new religious movements" are people seeking and questioning themselves. They are searching for a meaning to their life, attempting to satisfy their religious needs, to be recognized for what they are, to fill a void in their existence. They are wondering about the "how" and "why" of suffering and death; they want clear, precise, concrete and definitive answers to their questions. . . .

Furthermore, in the "global" society in which we live, where information and exchanges now circulate rapidly and freely, we discover the range of different religions. We observe that there is a wide variety of religious products available on "the great market of symbolism," that Christianity has "competitors" and that there are real opportunities to change religion or to give up for good the creed one has professed and practiced until now.

Most Rev. Pierre Raffin, Doc. 59

Before the question of meaning, the inhabitants of Europe find themselves facing a dilemma today. Marxism, violently imposed in Central and Eastern Europe, has collapsed and left many people with a void of meaning. On the other hand, practical materialism is widespread throughout Europe. In our cultural context many people conceive of their life, think and act *as if God did not exist*. At the same time, there is a lingering nostalgia for religious experience; nevertheless this often distances people from the authentic Christian faith. Young people in particular are easily drawn to new forms of religiosity and sects of various origins.

Episcopal Conference of Germany,
Commission for Faith, Doc. 51

The different expressions of the new religiosity are not a fringe phenomenon. They mainly affect precisely the centers of Western culture and thrive in the largest, richest cities of the northern hemisphere, often making use of considerable funds to spread also to the poorest regions in the South of the world. However, although this phenomenon demonstrates individual features, those, that is, of a society of images and communications, it must not be considered entirely unheard of since it already exists in the history of religions and in that of Christianity.

Episcopal Conference of Italy,
Secretariat for Ecumenism and Dialogue, Doc. 52

Middle East: Causes and Context

The change that has affected human societies has interrupted life's traditional rhythm. It has separated members of a single family from one another. Many people have the feeling they have lost their roots. It is this change that has caused the sects to flourish and spread. They claim to offer uprooted people what they need, such as human warmth and help to achieve their ambitions. . . . They are presented with a fresh view of themselves, of human beings, of history and of the cosmos, and they are promised the birth of a new world where their worries will come to an end.

Cardinal Nasrallah Pierre Sfeir, Doc. 61

Africa: Causes and Context

Our world is in a situation of real and deep crisis in every sphere. The result is the widespread vulnerability of the people of today in the form of cultural, social, moral, spiritual and financial crises.

Cultural crisis: This is in fact the most serious and the most important: it influences the whole of life. The world of today, because of the sophisticated means of transport and the mass media (radio, television, newspapers) is more and more a crossroads where the different cultures are obliged to meet. . . . We know that those who have the most efficient means to communicate their civilizations impose their own concepts of life upon the weakest, which bring a new form of slavery. The consequences are revolt, rejection and protection mechanisms.

Social crisis: our current society is lacerated. Even its basic structures are unsettled, for example, the family. Yesterday the lineage or clan was spoken of. Marriage considered as an institution was protected by laws, rules. . . . The custodians of the laws and the conduct prescribed for social harmony were the elders, the old. Today . . . the order and harmony of the village are turned upside down. Some religious movements would seem to be a protest in face of this disturbance and social harmony.

Moral and spiritual crisis: certain moral and spiritual criteria that regulate life in society and the relations between people are disintegrating, because of the introduction of new religions and a new moral code whose demands are not the same. . . .

Financial crisis: . . . The sects, offering a place where solidarity is truly practiced, become for the abandoned and the frustrated a protest against present day society that condemns some to poverty or undeserved suffering.

Episcopal Conference of Congo, Doc. 36

Americas: Causes and Context

The explanations offered for why the new religious movements arouse interest in some people are numerous and varied. Among them we should note:

• The ongoing and deepening social crisis, which arouses a certain collective anxiety and loss of identity and causes people to lose their roots.

• The ability these movements have to adapt to social circumstances and momentarily satisfy some needs of people. A taste for novelty certainly plays a role.

• The fact that the Church has become distant from some groups—whether poor or rich—who are seeking new channels of religious expression, but who also may be evading the commitments entailed in faith.

• Their ability to provide an apparent solution to the desires for "healing" on the part of people who are suffering.

IV General Conference of Latin American Bishops, Doc. 39

Causes that encourage the penetration of the sects in Venezuela:

a) their work methodology, which involves personal contact and continuous visits to homes as well as their presence in the most out-of-the-way places and sectors;

b) their concern for new members who discover that they are important, that they have a lead role and are members of a fraternal community;

c) their perseverance in the aggressive task of proselytism;

d) the emotional, participatory, carefree and personalized cult;

e) easy access to the Bible and biblical formation; conviction based on a biblical and doctrinal formation, which ends by influencing its members;

f) an abundance of aid from the United States and other countries.

Episcopal Conference of Venezuela, Doc. 43

The sponsorship of groups and institutions, foreign and national, sometimes motivated by financial, political or ideological aims; the legislation we are governed by that originated in the liberalism and positivism of the past century; and the lay school for the education of our children and young people.

Episcopal Conference of Mexico, Doc. 40

We observed in biblical fundamentalism an effort to try to find in the Bible all the direct answers for living—though the Bible itself nowhere claims such authority. The appeal of such an approach is understandable. . . . People of all ages yearn for answers. They look for sure, definite rules for living. And they are given answers—simplistic answers to complex issues—in a confident and enthusiastic way in fundamentalist Bible groups.

National Conference of Catholic Bishops
(United States), Doc. 41

2
DIVERSITY OF
ORIGIN OF THE MOVEMENTS

It is important to recognize certain distinctions and not to inaccurately group all movements together.

At least seven major headings can be suggested:

1) Fundamentalist biblical movements;
2) Groups with Christian origins, whose claims to orthodoxy are questionable;
3) Movements deriving from the great Asian religions;
4) Local prophetic foundations, often syncretist in character;
5) Gnostic-oriented groups, especially in the diversity of the New Age movement;
6) Philosophical or psychological groups, often of Western origin;
7) Pseudo-religious groups characterized by magic or occultist tendencies.

DOCUMENTS AND DISCOURSES OF POPE JOHN PAUL II

Distinct Backgrounds for Various Forms of NRMs

Some of these groups call themselves Christian; others take their inspiration from Eastern religions; others still echo some of the most revolutionary ideologies of our day.

Message for World Migration Day, Doc. 5

Connection of NRMs with Local Forms of Folklore, Superstition, or Popular Religiosity

Religious syncretism is a truly complex phenomenon, and has not yet been fully studied. With the development of industrialization in Brazil and the consequent internal migration from the country to the cities, the influence of *spiritualistic practices* becomes easier, as does folkloristic investigation, undertaken sometimes as a form of tourism, into the symbols, rites and popular festivities with which these new cults are maintained and developed. And the result is well known: certain mythic and demiurgic aspects arising from beliefs with the most diverse origins and meanings have intermingled in a confused fashion with the basic mysteries of Christian faith.

To the Bishops of the North-2 Region of Brazil, Doc. 4

Claims of Healings or Apparitions

Those who are set apart for the work of preaching (cf. Acts 13:2) must not fail to read the signs of the times, both positive and negative (cf. Nm 22-23). Significant among the latter is the growth of sects and other new religious movements, which often appeal to alleged apparitions, prophecies and miraculous cures. The attraction of these movements sometimes lies in their apparent success in responding to the spiritual needs of people—the hunger of their hearts for something deeper, for healing, consolation and contact with the transcendent.

To the Bishops of Ghana, Doc. 12

OTHER DOCUMENTS OF THE CHURCH

The Question of Terminology
"Sect"

The word "sect" seems to refer more directly to small groups that broke away from a major religious group, generally Christian, and that hold deviating beliefs or practices. . . . The word "sect" is not used in the same sense everywhere. In Latin America, for example, there is a tendency to apply the term to all non-Catholic groups, even when these are families of traditional Protestant churches. But even in Latin America, in circles that are more sensitive to ecumenism, the word "sect" is reserved for the more extremist or aggressive groups. In Western Europe the word has a negative connotation, while in Japan the new religions of Shinto or Buddhist origin are freely called sects in a non-derogatory sense.

Cardinal Francis Arinze, Doc. 25

"New Religious Movement"

The term "new religious movements" is more neutral than that of "sects" when referring to these groups. They are called "new" not only because they showed themselves in their present form after the Second World War, but also because they present themselves as alternatives to the institutional official religions and the prevailing culture. They are called "religious" because they profess to offer a vision of the religious or sacred world, or means to reach other objectives such as transcendental knowledge, spiritual illumination or self-realization, or because they offer to members their answers to fundamental questions.

Cardinal Francis Arinze, Doc. 25

"Sect" or "Church"?

It is important to keep clearly in view the distinction between sects and new religious movements on the one hand, and churches and ecclesial communities on the other. The tendency in some parts of the world to use the word "sect" for all non-Catholic groups is evidence of serious misunderstanding.

Cardinal Francis Arinze, Doc. 25

The question of the definition of those new movements or groups as distinct from *church* or *legitimate movements within a church* is a contentious matter. It will help to distinguish sects that find their origin in the Christian religion from those that come from another religious or humanitarian source. The matter becomes quite delicate when these groups are of Christian origin. Nevertheless, it is important to make this distinction. Indeed, certain sectarian mentalities and attitudes, i.e., attitudes of intolerance and aggressive proselytism, do not necessarily constitute a sect, nor do they suffice to characterize a sect. . . .

The criterion for distinguishing between *sects* of Christian origin, on the one hand, and *churches and ecclesial communities,* on the other hand, might be found in the sources of the teaching of these groups. For instance, sects could be those groups that, apart from the Bible, have other *revealed* books or *prophetic messages;* or groups that exclude from the Bible certain protocanonical books, or radically change their content.

Secretariat for Promoting Christian Unity,
Secretariat for Non-Christians,
Secretariat for Non-Believers,
and Pontifical Council for Culture, Doc. 23

Categorization

With reference to background knowledge system: Four types can be distinguished.

There are movements based on Holy Scripture. These are therefore Christian or they are derived from Christianity.

A second group of NRMs are those derived from other religions such as Hinduism, Buddhism or traditional religions. Some of them assume in a syncretistic way elements coming from Christianity.

A third group of sects show signs of a decomposition of the genuine idea of religion and of a return of paganism. . . . They show signs of a culture that is getting spiritually lazy or tired in front of the exaggerated rationalism of modern technological civilizations.

A fourth set of sects are gnostic. In their naturalistic claims, they seem to offer to free people from the weight of freedom and responsibility, and launch them on a road that does not demand moral decisions from them but only offers them "illumination."

Cardinal Francis Arinze, Doc. 25

With reference to Christianity: From the doctrinal point of view, the NRMs that operate in traditionally Christian regions can be located in four categories insofar as they distance themselves from the Christian vision of the world: those that reject the Church, those that reject Christ, those that reject the role of God (and yet maintain a generic sense of "religion"), and those that reject the role of religion (and maintain a sense of the sacred, but manipulated by man to acquire power over others or the cosmos).

Cardinal Francis Arinze, Doc. 25

NRMs in the Americas

Fundamentalist sects are religious groups that insist that only faith in Jesus Christ saves, that the only basis for faith is Scripture interpreted personally in a fundamentalist manner, and hence excluding the Church; they emphasize the end of the world and the proximity of judgment.

*IV General Conference of
Latin American Bishops, Doc. 39*

New religious movements:
Several currents or kinds of phenomena can be distinguished:
- Para-Christian or semi-Christian forms, such as the Jehovah's Witnesses and Mormons. Each of these movements has its own characteristics, but they share a proselytizing approach, millenarianism, and an organizational style similar to those of businesses.
- Esoteric forms that seek special enlightenment and share secret items of knowledge and a religious concern for the occult. Such

is the case of spiritist, Rosicrucian, gnostic, theosophical, and similar currents.

- Philosophies and kinds of worship that have some oriental aspects but are rapidly adapting to our continent, such as *Hare Krishna*, Divine Light, *Ananda Marga,* and others, which offer mysticism and a communal experience.
- Groups that spring from the great Asian religions, whether Buddhism (e.g., *Seicho no Ié*), Hinduism (e.g., *Yoga*), or Islam (e.g., *Baha'i*), which are not only a manifestation of immigrants from Asia but are also taking root in some sectors of our society.
- Socio-religious enterprises, like the Moon sect or the New Acropolis, which have clear ideological and political aims along with their religious expressions . . . .
- A vast array of centers for "divine healing," which deal with the spiritual or physical ills of people who have problems or are poor. These therapeutic cults serve their clients individually.

IV General Conference of
Latin American Bishops, Doc. 39

New Age:

The New Age movement might be described as a quasi-religious subculture that is widespread but not in any way sharply defined. It is said to aim at making individuals come in touch with the light of their inner self and all manifestations of the divine inside and around them through a variety of exercises or techniques involving the mind. Actually, the New Age movement does not conceive of a personal God. God is within everyone. New Agers refer to this as a "good-force" or "pure consciousness". . . .

New Age calls for a radical shift in the way one looks at life: It questions our Western, scientific approach to things and proposes an Eastern, quasi-magical intuitive path. The bedrock of New Age thought is the fulfillment of human potential with the end result of ushering in the "Age of Aquarius."

Most Rev. Edward Anthony McCarthy, Doc. 46

NRMs in Europe

In this phenomenon of new religiosity, long-standing groups by now established and characterized by the force of their proselytism and anti-Catholic polemics converge from the point of view of the social dynamic. Although some of these have a Christian matrix, like the Jehovah's Witnesses who spread in Italy after the Second World War, they have drifted so far from genuine faith in Jesus

Christ, the Son of God, that they scarcely deserve to be called Christians.

More recently they have been joined by movements deriving from the Asian religions or with a syncretistic orientation that promise recipes for peace and inner happiness as well as movements that focus on the development of human potential, while nevertheless preserving some religious aspects. The ancient esoteric-occultist trend has re-emerged and split into many small groups whose influence goes way beyond the circle of the initiated, thanks to the commercial distribution methods often practiced.

Episcopal Conference of Italy,
Secretariat for Ecumenism and Dialogue, Doc. 52

NRMs in Africa

Africa is characterized by a great variety of sects and religious movements of diverse origin: [Christian-based groups] coming for the most part from North America; Western, non-Christian philosophies of life; new religious movements with their origin in the East, some of which entered the world scene because they have first been implanted in North America; movements of Islamic inspiration. The thousands of "African independent churches," mainly offshoots of missionary churches and bearing certain aspects of African traditional religion, represent a confused picture: some are clearly to be regarded as "ecclesial bodies," while others seem to have all the characteristics of sects properly so-called. Some groups within the Church degenerate into sects.

Synod of Bishops:
Special Assembly for Africa, Doc. 35

3
IMPACT AND PROCESS
OF COMMUNICATION

The success of the NRMs is due not only to sociocultural causes or to spiritual aspirations that do not find answers; it can also be attributed in large measure to the process of communication adopted and to strategies of spreading influence.

In pastoral documents, the methods used by the NRMs are frequently criticized. A recurring complaint is that some movements adopt methods of recruiting that lack respect for human freedom and that therefore can be called "proselytism" or indoctrination. These can range from intense psychological pressures to financial inducements to join a particular movement. In addition, many groups distort the truth of the Catholic Church and make prejudiced attacks against aspects of its religious practices and teachings.

Many NRM "preachers" are expert in communicating a simple and sometimes emotional message and in using the new media as instruments in their campaigns. Thus the success of such groups sometimes depends on uniting subjective and objective attractions: meeting the spiritual hungers of people by means of sophisticated methods of persuasion.

Hence a discernment is needed between those methods that provide a healthy challenge to the Church and those dangerous methods that ignore the right to objective information, to freedom of conscience, and in general the right of each person to dignity and respect.

The strategies of communication target particular categories of people. Not everyone is equally liable to be attracted to these movements. In general the most likely candidates are people who are weak in various ways: those who are psychologically fragile, those whose Christian formation has been poor, those in problematic moral or family situations, the young without strong roots in family or any tradition, and those who for various reasons have difficulties with the Church.

It is important also to note that the type of communication used by the NRMs will differ depending on the type of movement in question, and that the categories of people targeted are not equally vulnerable to all kinds of NRMs.

DOCUMENTS AND DISCOURSES OF POPE JOHN PAUL II

Aggressive Mode of Communication

The almost aggressive zeal with which certain people seek new recruits by going from house to house or stopping passersby at street corners is a bogus sectarian version of apostolic missionary zeal; the attention shown the individual and the importance given to his or her contribution to the cause and the growth of the religious group does not stem from the desire to make good use of one's own life by feeling useful to the community to which a person belongs, but rather constitutes a deformed expression of the active role that is proper to believers, living members of Christ's body, called to work for the spread of God's Kingdom.

Message for World Migration Day, Doc. 5

Nor does the Church close her eyes to the danger of fanaticism or fundamentalism among those who, in the name of an ideology that purports to be scientific or religious, claim the right to impose on others their own concept of what is true and good. *Christian truth* is not of this kind. Since it is not an ideology, the Christian faith does not presume to imprison changing sociopolitical realities in a rigid schema, and it recognizes that human life is realized in history in conditions that are diverse and imperfect. Furthermore, in constantly reaffirming the transcendent dignity of the person, the Church's method is always that of respect for freedom.

Centesimus annus §46, Doc. 8

Tendency to Promise Immediate Solutions to Problems

. . . the growth of sects and other new religious movements, which often appeal to alleged apparitions, prophecies and miraculous cures. The attraction of these movements sometimes lies in their apparent success in responding to the spiritual needs of people— the hunger of their hearts for something deeper, for healing, consolation and contact with the transcendent.

To the Bishops of Ghana, Doc. 12

As these persons and families meet very new situations and enter into quite different environments that often are foreign and even hostile to them, with their values and ways of living and thinking, they bring with them a Christian formation that is still very fragile, a faith still so very weak and already beset by growing secularization; they do not find the necessary pastoral help, and with the impact of the consumer society and the mass media's pressure they become, clearly, easy game for the fanaticism of the sects. Certain sects are characterized by the aggressiveness of their proselytism; others offer to the unwary the illusion of having an immediate answer for their enormous spiritual, emotional and even material needs.

To the Bishops of the North-2 Region of Brazil, Doc. 4

Lack of Growth into Christian Maturity as a Vulnerability to Proselytism

We must humbly acknowledge that in certain cases the baptized have not yet, for whatever reason, discovered the fulfillment of these needs in the mystery of the Incarnate Word entrusted to the Church.

To the Bishops of Ghana, Doc. 12

Targeting of People from Certain Cultural Backgrounds

Your ministry must take account of the richness of religious expression and cultural diversity that characterizes the Hispanic community and demands appropriate pastoral programs and initiatives. Among the principal pastoral tasks in relation to the Hispanic community is that of evangelization and catechesis, especially in the face of extremely active proselytism by other religious groups.

To the Bishops of Alaska, Arkansas, Idaho,
Montana, Oklahoma, Oregon, Texas, and
Washington (United States), Doc. 15

OTHER DOCUMENTS OF THE CHURCH

The Appeal of NRMs: Sign of Valid Aspirations or Ambiguous?

The sects offer people a closed community that is more fraternal than the Catholic masses. Worship is participative and simpler. Biblical fundamentalism makes the initiates feel that they are learned in religion because they memorize some passages from the Bible. Their consciences are assuaged because God directly forgives sins. There are no complications about abortion and birth control. Some groups regularize second marriages between divorced people. These characteristics of the sects attract new members and, at the same time, make them fanatical.

Cardinal Ernesto Corripio Ahumada, Doc. 26

There is a need for a sense of community, and sects offer human warmth, aid and attention to the person, especially to people who are divorced, who are migrants, alcoholics.

Many people feel a need to come to terms with themselves, to feel safe, secure, able to overcome their problems and complexes; sects offer a palpable religious experience. . . .

People need to feel recognized, to improve their social status, to be taken into account; what sects offer people is interest in them as persons, offering them a share of responsibility and inviting them to become part of a select group.

People need spiritual direction: the sect offers them this through the pastor, the religious leader.

Cardinal Miguel Obando Bravo, Doc. 28

The rapid expansion of these sects in certain parts of the world, including the Gulf, is in great measure due to the psychological, social and economic conditions prevailing in these regions. It is no less the result of their missionary fervor and the efficiency of their method. They follow a process of simple techniques perfected by years of experience.

At first they *work on the emotional plane.* The new immigrant is taken notice of. Warmth and friendship are given to him. He feels he is esteemed and appreciated. He is made to feel that his talents have a contribution to make for the advent of God's kingdom. This personal approach is hard to resist.

Next comes *the phase of indoctrination.* Some of the immigrant's beliefs are called in question. Doubts are thrown in. Adherents to these sects have only a very superficial knowledge of theology, or Scripture, but they are specialists in a limited field. Their topics of attack, and their quotations from Scripture are the same for the last 400 years. Their "myths" and "fables" have been exposed over and over again, but they keep on repeating them so as to ensnare the ignorant and innocent.

This phase of brainwashing when the prospective adherent is subjected to a barrage of scriptural quotations, indoctrination, slogans, isolation, social and psychological pressures, and a climate of fear and insecurity, leave him completely confused and helpless.

Most Rev. Giovanni Bernardo Gremoli, Doc. 60

Commercial travelers peddling salvation are increasing on our roads and reach the remotest villages in our provinces, offering their wares as the latest and best bargain for man's happiness, the new truth that must sweep away everything that existed previously. Badly informed Christians, spurred on by the longing for unclouded bliss, let themselves be taken for a ride.

Most Rev. Robert Sastre, Doc. 38

Not all methods deserve to be frowned upon. The dynamism of their missionary drive, the evangelistic responsibility assigned to the new "converts," their use of the mass media and their setting of the objectives to be attained, should make us ask ourselves questions as to how to make more dynamic the missionary activity of the Church.

There are methods used by some NRMs that are contrary to the spirit of the Gospel because these methods do not respect human freedom of conscience sufficiently.

Cardinal Francis Arinze, Doc. 25

Characterization of Proselytism

Proselytism: Here is meant improper attitudes and behavior in the practice of Christian witness. Proselytism embraces whatever violates the right of the human person, Christian or non-Christian, to be free from external coercion in religious matters, or whatever in the proclamation of the Gospel does not conform to the ways God draws free men to himself in response to his calls to serve in spirit and in truth.

Cited in The National Pastoral Plan for Hispanic Ministry, *Doc. 42*

[The fundamentalist sects] are characterized by their very enthusiastic proselytizing through persistent house visiting and large-scale distribution of bibles, magazines, and books; their presence and the opportunistic help they provide at times of personal or family crisis; and their great technical skill in using the media. They have at their disposal immense funding from other countries and the tithes they oblige all their members to pay.

Other features are a rigorous moralism, prayer meetings with a participatory and emotional Bible-based worship, and their aggressive stance toward the Church; they often resort to defamation and to material inducements. Although they are only weakly committed to the temporal realm, they tend to become involved in politics with a view to taking power.

IV General Conference of Latin American Bishops, Doc. 39

The fundamentalist groups come with a financially well-backed plan. Millions of dollars flow easily in different forms, such as funding for livelihood projects, educational scholarships, career enhancement programs, employment, etc. Some of them . . . openly pay their members for every "conversion" they obtain and the jobs they provide for their members, thus offering them a certain economic security.

Cardinal Ricardo J. Vidal, Doc. 31

It is usually said that proselytism is an activity aiming to win over the proselytized which uses an indiscreet zeal that moves people to convince others of their own beliefs. It is the reckless search for adepts merely for the purpose of increasing numbers and, with the help of dishonest and anti-evangelical means, exploiting poverty: for example, buying support or exercising unjustifiable pressure, intimidating by the use of psychological alienation and brainwashing. . . . It is the action directed at procuring adepts for a religious creed, violating their freedom.

Most Rev. Javier Lozano Barragán, Doc. 45

Psychological Pressure of Some NRMs

Some recruitment, training techniques, and indoctrination procedures practiced by a number of sects and cults, which often are highly sophisticated, partly account for their success. Those most often attracted by such measures are those who, firstly, do not know that the approach is often staged, and, secondly, are unaware of the nature of the contrived conversion and training methods (the social and psychological manipulation) to which they are subjected. The sects often impose their own norms of thinking, feeling, and behaving. This is in contrast to the Church's approach, which implies full-capacity informed consent.

Secretariat for Promoting Christian Unity,
Secretariat for Non-Christians,
Secretariat for Non-Believers,
and Pontifical Council for Culture, Doc. 23

The existence has been denounced in these sects of indefensible attitudes and various manipulative techniques used on individuals who come to these organizations seeking something, or fleeing the emptiness they find in our society, our families and sometimes, our churches: for example, the exploitation of the Bible by means of a fundamentalist and fragmented interpretation, out of context; the abuse of emotional experiences, fanaticizing adepts to the point of bringing them to a state of alienation and marginalization; the use of the total isolation of individuals away from all external influence; adopting methods that undermine mental health and lead to intellectual confusion, spreading guilt complexes and destroying critical thought or reflection.

Episcopal Conference of Spain,
Commission for Interconfessional Relations, Doc. 53

Differences among NRMs in Methods of Communication and Targeted Recruits

The missionary activity of these groups is directed at attracting the attention of the sectors to which the Church pays the least attention, and persons with little religious training. Thus it offers them more personalized and constant attention, as a possibility of an ongoing religious and biblical formation. . . .

There is also a drive to attract the attention of nominal, non-practicing middle-class Catholics, where religious ignorance is rife. It is not surprising to find in these movements persons belonging to professional classes and of greater means. University youth and professional groups exist which carry out constant activities in their respective sectors.

Some groups seek adepts in the middle-to-upper and professional classes. Likewise, young people are offered the possibility of filling their leisure with sports and cultural activities that disguise a proselytizing interest. Groups inspired by the Eastern religions and by a certain type of philosophy (Rosicrucian, gnostic, metaphysical, *Hare Krishna* groups, etc.) seek people with a certain cultural level or a natural taste for the esoteric.

Lastly, it should not be forgotten that these groups seek to capture people who have psychological and moral problems, who have difficult relations with the Church, who have suffered because of bad example, or who are searching for help for their moral regeneration.

Episcopal Conference of Venezuela, Doc. 43

If a closer look is taken at what the NRMs are offering to Western society, it will be seen that some of them are essentially therapeutic in nature, appealing to the individual and showing little concern for the general welfare of society. Others however have a more universalist outlook, and these attract people of a more active nature and altruistic bent. In spreading their message they make use of the modern means of communication whose rapidity and power have brought about such a degree of interdependence in the world of today.

There is a fascination in the aims proposed by this second group: the unity of the world (sometimes exalted as Mother Earth, *Gaia*), the bringing of a new era, the awakening of a new planetary consciousness. These are to be achieved in spiritual communion with like-minded people, all those who are fellow-pilgrims along the way. Indeed the proposed horizons often go beyond this world and take on a metahistorical and metaspiritual character.

Most Rev. Michael L. Fitzgerald, Doc. 32

It would seem that the groups most at risk would be mainly those in some difficulty with the Church and those far removed from the presence of the priest. Youths looking for security or "knowledge" or what is "new" are particularly vulnerable; so are women and those who feel isolated in urban areas and in the peripheries of cities. Their particular attraction for women could be because of their appeal to the emotions and the fact that women are admitted to most offices. People may be attracted by their offers of healing, bodily and spiritual, or by the promises of instant solutions to all problems. Some sects pose as channels of professional advancement and economic success. Others emphasize a narrow spiritual conversion that ignores or even rejects social and political responsibility.

Synod of Bishops: Special Assembly for Africa, Doc. 35

4
SPIRITUAL AND THEOLOGICAL DISCERNMENT

The pastoral documents on the NRMs note that because of the context of religious pluralism in which many Christians find themselves today and because of the weakening of belonging to the faith community, some people attempt to harmonize all religions or to insert into their own creed elements that clash with the Christian message. Others again, while wishing to remain faithful to the teachings of the Church, find themselves confused by the propaganda of certain movements and feel the need for clear principles of theological and spiritual discernment.

These pastoral texts contain, therefore, principles of discernment on the main doctrines taught by the more widespread movements, such as those marked by a fundamentalist interpretation of the Bible or those who adhere to the general myth of the New Age. Moreover, they comment on deviant tendencies of modern religiosity, noting instances where the sense of truth is lost or replaced with a vague spiritualism, where the notion of salvation through Jesus Christ is questioned, and where the eschatological waiting is emptied of meaning.

Especially with evangelical groups there is also an almost universal tendency to attack important aspects of Catholic life, such as sacraments or devotion to Mary or the saints. This goes hand in hand with devaluing the role of church in general and of tradition as opposed to Scripture.

Among syncretistic groups a frequent problem arises from a belief in reincarnation, a doctrine that seems to have many adherents among the new generations of Europe in particular. Answering it involves a genuine understanding of the dignity of each person before God and an appreciation of our sharing in the resurrection of Christ.

Another potential source of theological confusion stems from the trend to seek methods of spirituality and of meditation from outside the Christian tradition. This tendency together with the whole New Age approach is in danger of a Pelagian emphasis on self-salvation and a forgetfulness of the mediation and gift of Christ.

We can find in some NRMs the tendency to replace the person and doctrine of Christ with some other psychological or doctrinal focus: the personality of a charismatic leader, the self-realization of the individual, the quest for the extraordinary, emotional experiences of an intense kind, or the distorted or ideological interpretation of Scripture.

In some movements one finds a preponderance of magical elements that, rooted in the desire to exalt man and his power, stray from the field of authentic religious experience.

DOCUMENTS AND DISCOURSES OF POPE JOHN PAUL II

Salvation as Sectarian Monopoly; Sacred as Magical

In these movements salvation is considered to be a prerogative of only a small group, led by superior individuals, who believe they have a special relationship with a God whose secrets only they claim to know. Their search for the sacred itself takes on an ambiguous form. For some of them it is a search for higher values towards which man strives without ever being able to attain them; for others it is situated within the realm of the magical; they try to draw it within their own sphere to manipulate it and make it serve their purposes.

Message for World Migration Day, Doc. 5

In the context of your mission as educators in the faith, you perceive the need for respectful yet clear spiritual discernment with regard to the "syncretist and esoteric" groups that are particularly active in many parts of the country. *Popular piety* itself needs to be purified of an excessive leaning towards the "mysterious" and "magical" as far as extraordinary happenings are concerned, which seem to exceed the limits of the human mind.

To the Bishops of Venezuela, Doc. 2

False Prophets and Promotion of a Deceptive Spiritualism

There are *false prophets* and *false teachers of how to live.* First of all there are those who teach people to leave the body, time and space in order to be able to enter into what they call "true life." They condemn creation, and in the name of a deceptive spirituality they lead thousands of young people along the paths of an impossible liberation, which eventually leaves them even more isolated, victims of their own illusions and of the evil in their own lives.

Seemingly at the opposite extreme, there are the teachers of the "fleeting moment," who invite people to give free rein to every instinctive urge or longing, with the result that individuals fall prey to a sense of anguish and anxiety leading them to seek refuge in false artificial paradises, such as that of drugs.

And there are those who teach that the meaning of life lies solely in the quest for success, the accumulation of wealth, the development of personal abilities, without regard for the needs of others or respect for values, at times not even for the fundamental value of life itself.

These and other kinds of false teachers of life, also numerous in the modern world, propose goals that not only fail to bring satisfaction but often intensify and exacerbate the thirst that burns in the human heart.

Message for the VIII World Youth Day, Doc. 10

Distortion of the Christian Understanding of Revelation and Redemption

In their syncretistic and immanent outlook, these parareligious movements pay little heed to revelation, and instead try to come to God through knowledge and experience based on elements borrowed from Eastern spirituality or from psychological techniques. They tend to relativize religious doctrine, in favor of a vague worldview expressed as a system of myths and symbols dressed in religious language. Moreover, they often propose a pantheistic concept of God that is incompatible with sacred Scripture and Christian tradition. They replace personal responsibility to God for our actions with a sense of duty to the cosmos, thus overturning the true concept of sin and the need for redemption through Christ.

To the Bishops of Iowa, Kansas, Missouri,
and Nebraska (United States), Doc. 13

Reduction of Christianity to a Natural Level

To neglect the supernatural dimension of the Christian life is to empty of meaning the mystery of Christ and of the Church. . . . Nevertheless, it is a sad fact that some Christians today are succumbing to the temptation "to reduce Christianity to merely human wisdom, a pseudo-science of well-being" (*Redemptoris missio* no. 11). To preach a version of Christianity that benignly ignores, when it does not explicitly deny, that our ultimate hope is the "resurrection of the body and life everlasting" (Apostles' Creed) runs counter to revelation and the whole of Catholic tradition.

To the Bishops of Iowa, Kansas, Missouri,
and Nebraska (United States), Doc. 13

Tertio millenio adveniente

The importance of proclaiming a new Christian eschatology is underlined throughout the letter Tertio millenio adveniente. *Among other things, the spread of belief in reincarnation is mentioned.*

> In man there is an irrepressible longing to live forever. How are we to imagine a life beyond death? Some have considered various forms of *reincarnation:* depending on one's previous life, one would receive a new life in either a higher or lower form, until purification is attained. This belief, deeply rooted in some Eastern religions, itself indicates that man rebels against the finality of death. He is convinced that his nature is essentially spiritual and immortal.
>
> Christian revelation excludes reincarnation, and speaks of a fulfillment that man is called to achieve in the course of a single earthly existence. Man achieves this fulfillment of his destiny through the sincere gift of self, a gift that is made possible only through his encounter with God. . . .
>
> Tertio millenio adveniente, *no. 9, Doc. 16*

Inculturation and Syncretism

> It is certain that we must esteem and respect legitimate religious traditions, for example, those which are authentically African. . . . However, it would be quite another thing to welcome them and incorporate them into the content of the Christian message. This we would not be able to do without careful discernment. It is necessary to duly purify all elements that, for example, are clearly incompatible with the mystery of the oneness and absolute transcendence of a personal God, or connected with the economy of salvation, in which Christ is the only way for people to be redeemed; it is good to recall as well all the topics regarding the demands of Christian moral law.
>
> *To the Bishops of the North-2 Region of Brazil, Doc. 4*

Veritatis splendor

Even if the encyclical Veritatis splendor *does not speak explicitly of the "new religiosity," it contains valuable principles for discernment that apply to these as to other expressions of modern culture. Thus, in the introduction and chapter 1 we see how the search for the meaning of life is a call towards the truth and goodness that has its foundation in God. No darkness can totally eliminate in man the light of God the Creator and the longing for his truth and knowledge (cf.*

nos. 7-9). In other articles the link between truth/goodness and man's freedom is explained (cf. nos. 31-35).

Reason and experience not only confirm the weakness of human freedom; they also confirm its tragic aspects. Man comes to realize that his freedom is in some mysterious way inclined to betray this openness to the True and the Good, and that all too often he actually prefers to choose finite, limited and ephemeral goods. What is more, within his errors and negative decisions, man glimpses the source of a deep rebellion, which leads him to reject the Truth and the Good in order to set himself up as an absolute principle unto himself: "You will be like God" (Gen 3:5).

Veritatis splendor, no. 86, Doc. 14

OTHER DOCUMENTS OF THE CHURCH

Doctrinal Relativism as Precursor to "Sects"

The spread of sects and the challenge they present to the Church have theological as well as pastoral implications. Doctrinal confusion regarding the content of the faith opens the way to the proliferation of sects, to their practical justification, and above all, to a lack of commitment in pastoral care and the explicit proclamation of Jesus Christ, which establishes the Christian community.

There is a gnostic relativism and a theological misunderstanding that levels all religions, different religious experiences and beliefs, to a least common denominator in which everything is the same and each person can take an equally valid road to salvation.

There are some theological theories that empty and deform the revealed mystery of the Word Incarnate in Jesus Christ, and that arbitrarily construct the divine mystery that "is emerging," "is being incarnated" in various religious types (incarnations, saviors, mediators, revealers, founders, mystics).

Cardinal Jozef Tomko, Doc. 30

Necessity for Consistent Faith When Encountering Believers of Other Religions

Interreligious dialogue, which in the perspective of the Second Vatican Council is strictly linked with the Church's evangelizing mission, must also rely on a consistent and integral conception and expression of the truth of the Christian faith. . . .

Keeping firmly anchored in the basic truths of the faith, far from jeopardizing dialogue, we make it genuine, possible and fruitful, for the knowledge of the truth.

Episcopal Conference of Italy,
Secretariat for Ecumenism and Dialogue, Doc. 52

Necessity of Faith in Jesus Christ as the Unique Redeemer of Humankind

Facing the phenomenon of religious pluralism and also of the sects and new religious movements, we can find sometimes interpretations and attitudes that deeply reduce the Christian truth. In particular, the opinion can be spread that Jesus Christ is only one of the many manifestations of the Word of God in the religious history of humanity; or that the Holy Spirit is none other than the Christian name of a universal "divine spirit," witnessed in various religious experiences; or again, that the Church should be put in parentheses, in favor of a vague concept of God's kingdom that creates a brotherhood of all religions.

These tendencies are unacceptable from the point of view of the Christian faith, because more or less consciously they do not recognize the singularity of Jesus Christ, and therefore neither his uniqueness nor the central place in the work of salvation. They have an erroneous concept of the Holy Spirit and of the Trinitarian mystery, and they neglect or refuse the Church as a universal means of salvation.

Episcopal Conference of Italy,
Secretariat for Ecumenism and Dialogue, Doc. 52

As regards the values that new religious groups have to offer . . . we said that they must be purified and completed in this deep light. We do not find salvation merely through the sum of worldly truths— whose total we could call "Divine Logos" by virtue of the exemplarity of Creation—but only through the concrete Son of God who is our God and our Truth, specifically through his paschal incarnation, and whose name is Christ, Jesus of Nazareth.

The mystery is not necessarily something indistinct, nebulous and vague, but the dazzling luminosity of the divine marvel that divinizes us in a most concrete way, definitive and unrepeatable: through the paschal incarnation of the Word, the Logos, the Son of God. The Holy Spirit is not a stray force in the universe . . . , but the love of the Father and the Son who was sent to our hearts to call God the Father "Father," since he united us through divine love to the Son of God in such a way that we call ourselves and are children of God.

Most Rev. Javier Lozano Barragán, Doc. 45

Uniqueness of the Incarnation of Christ

A concept deriving from the Hindu tradition, present—explicitly or implicitly—in the new religiosity, can help us to focus better on this most important point: it is the concept of *avatâra*. This is a Sanskrit term that literally means "descent." It is applied to the divinity and to his condescending manifestation in the sphere of the tangible (not only human). Many Hindu experts and occultists translate it simply by "incarnation." Here then we have the central dogma of Christianity channeled into a broader historical and religious category. The god Vishnu's "descents" are supposed to have been frequent. His last human apparition is supposed to have been Krishna. The event of Christ thus becomes only the particular case of a more general category. A case that can be repeated again, as for example, is claimed for the Indian *guru*, Satya Sai Baba.

In fact, a more careful examination, theological such as the subject requires, immediately shows that the concepts of *avatâra* and incarnation can be linked only by virtue of a serious error. Apart from the historical inconsistency of the figure of Krishna, the human manifestation of God is resolved in the assumption of an apparent body. Whoever applies this concept to Christ falls more or less consciously into the errors of an ancient heresy, Docetism (from the Greek *dokeô:* "to appear") and certainly does not express the Christian faith. The Christian incarnation, which implies the truth and completeness of Jesus' humanity, emerges from this comparison as a unique and unrepeatable event, a true "sign of contradiction" (Lk 2:34) that does not sustain any syncretistic or pseudo-gnostic homologation, but requires a clear and decisive stance.

Most Rev. Giuseppe Casale, Doc. 55

The One Christ and the One Salvation

Christ cannot be confiscated by anyone. Since he is both Man and God, he goes beyond the limits of time and space and could not be imprisoned even within the boundaries of the Church he himself founded. And nevertheless he said: "If anyone says to you then, 'Look, here is the Christ,' or, 'Look, he is there,' do not believe it, for false Christs and false prophets will arise and produce signs and portents to deceive the elect, if that were possible. You therefore must be on your guard. I have forewarned you of everything" (Mk 13:21-23).

No one can create his own Christ or meet Christ at the turning in the path forged by his own fears, needs, frustrations, psychoses. Faith is not blind trust in a charismatic man. We do not have to adhere to a Christ of human invention, but to the Christ of the Gospels who came to witness to the Truth. Now what Christ is presented to us by the sects and esoteric movements that are on the increase among us? What salvation does he offer us?

God knows the extent to which people in our land are seeking salvation, even a salvation that never, for many of them, goes beyond purely earthly horizons. St. Paul spoke "with tears" of those who were "behaving as enemies of the cross of Christ," who only "think earthly things important" (Phil 3:18-19). He also speaks to us of people who "far from being content with sound teaching . . . will be avid for the latest novelty and collect themselves a whole series of teachers according to their own tastes; and then instead of listening to the truth, they will turn to myths" (2 Tm 4:3-4).

Most Rev. Robert Sastre, Doc. 38

The Type of Salvation Offered by Jesus Christ

The salvation that Jesus Christ brings us is not limited only to physical healing, but consists above all in the forgiveness of sins and the *liberation of the three human lusts:* money, the flesh and power. . . .

As Son of God, Jesus Christ introduces us into the universe of grace making us participants of divine life. By his death and resurrection, he opens to the very heart of our death the way of eternal life. While advancing towards eternal life, the Christian saves all the great earthly realities from corruption. Freeing himself from the concupiscence of the flesh, he saves love and the family. Freeing himself from the lust for money, he saves work and encourages sharing. Freeing himself from the lust for power, he frees social functions for a better service to the human community.

Episcopal Conference of Congo, Doc. 36

The Church as Mediatrix of Salvation and Guardian of Revealed Doctrine

In the Church and through her, man is given the opportunity to know God the Father, the Son and the Holy Spirit, and to participate in the divine life. In fact, Christ "endowed the Church, his

Body, with the fullness of the benefits and means of salvation; the Holy Spirit dwells in her, enlivens her with his gifts and charisms, sanctifies, guides and constantly renews her. The result is a unique and special relationship that, while not excluding the action of Christ and the Spirit outside the Church's visible boundaries, confers upon her a specific and necessary role" (*Redemptoris missio,* no. 18).

Episcopal Conference of Italy,
Secretariat for Ecumenism and Dialogue, Doc. 52

Christian revelation does not therefore derive from individual dreams, nor from inspirations left to the human imagination. It comes to us through the Judeo-Christian tradition handed down from generation to generation, under the vigilant gaze of the Church that has been guaranteed the help of the Holy Spirit who leads to the complete truth (cf. Jn 16:13).

This revelation preserves all the truth that our customs and the wisdom of our forefathers contain and enables us to make the most of them. It is not the custom which discerns the Gospel; it is the Gospel which discerns the custom. The first place where humanity's salvation is realized is in the conscience of each human being.

God's kingdom is within us (cf. Lk 17:21); but to share in the sources of salvation, each person is asked to prepare his conscience to listen, in order to accept the news of salvation proclaimed in the Church.

Episcopal Conference of Congo, Doc. 36

Disagreements as Foreseen by Christ and Manifest from the Beginning of the Church

The phenomenon of dissidence has not escaped the vision of Christ, who knows what man is and what there is within man. The Christian tradition has always interpreted in this way what Christ said in his prayer after the last Supper (priestly prayer) which is recounted in the fourth Gospel. . . .

According to Christ, in times of crisis, the phenomenon will be manifest with even greater keenness (cf. Mt 24:4-26; Mk 13:19-23). . . .

Those who want to read the Acts of the Apostles, Paul's Epistles, John's Revelation, with just a hint of foresight, already feel the wind of dissidence blowing. Sects are no longer mentioned, but the division of believers is already spreading its tentacles (cf. 1 Cor 1:10-13; 2 Cor 6:14ff, 12:20ff; Gal 1:6-9, 4:17ff; 1 Thes 1:3ff, 1:18-20; 2 Thes 2:16ff). . . .

I answered a chief . . . who came to ask me why there are divisions in the Church, that they are one of the consequences of the spirit of evil and sin that is in us, a result of man's pride.

Most Rev. Robert Sastre, Doc. 38

"From Their Fruits You Will Know Them" (Mt 7:20)

"What the Spirit brings is very different," St. Paul said, adding a verifiable list: "love, joy, peace, patience, kindness, goodness, trustfulness, gentleness and self-control" (Gal 5:22). In this light, discernment can be described simply as the art of judging the roots on the bases of the durability of the results.

More concretely, a series of questions can be suggested, which a person should ask himself every time he finds he has to face the need to discern the spiritual way he is about to take. The general aim is to discover whether the orientation taken is in harmony with the values of Christ's Gospel. The positive answers to these questions indicate fidelity to Christian roots, while the negative ones warn that there is deception and that what now appears good in the short term, could bring harm in the end. Does all this lead to compassion, humility, generosity or to selfishness and even pride? This really is a crucial question. The stream of life is either directed to one's neighbor, particularly to those who have been hurt by the world, towards the "lowliest" or towards one's own self. Involvement in some of the new forms of spirituality seems suspect precisely on this point, because in reality, rather than learning love, there is an underlying form of narcissism.

Cardinal Paul Poupard, Doc. 33

Response to Biblical Fundamentalism

We note especially the following errors that we cannot admit:

1. We cannot admit that God's revelation can be found only in the Bible. There was already revelation before any single line of the Bible was written. In the case of the New Testament, one need only recall that its earliest book (1 Thessalonians) was written about 20 years after Christ's death and resurrection. And yet the first Christians were not deprived of the Gospel of Christ. . . .

2. We cannot admit that the Bible by itself is a sufficient guide to know God's truth. . . . We need an authoritative interpreter of the word of God and that interpreter is the Church, which the Lord commissioned to teach and to which he promised the assistance of the Holy Spirit (cf. Mt 28:19; Jn 14:26, 16:13). The truth is, the Bible is not only God's word but a book produced by God through

the Church, and should never be separated from, and much less used against, the faith of the Church that gave it birth.

3. We cannot admit the minimizing of the role of the Church in salvation. . . . Only Christ saves, yes, but as Saul learned on his way to Damascus, Jesus identifies himself with the Church (cf Acts 9:4-5), which is his body (cf. 1 Cor 12:12; Eph 5:30).

Episcopal Conference of the Philippines, Doc. 49

The fundamentalist stance of literal interpretation of Scripture by each believer violates the history and tradition of Scripture. That is the danger. We also believe that fundamentalism constitutes a grave temptation . . . for it offers:

a) An unreasonable certainty about the meaning of Scripture texts regardless of their context.

b) An overly simplistic certainty of salvation, achieved instantaneously upon acceptance of Christ as savior.

c) A deep sense of personal security, in often identifying the "American way" with God's call and will.

d) Intimacy with God in a relationship so personal that it effectively excludes others.

Bishops of Alabama and Mississippi
(United States), Doc. 44

Fundamentalists, because of their literalist mindset, have often led others, by using brief Scripture quotations taken out of context, to world views and judgments very much opposed to our Catholic understanding. They set up an exaggerated contrast between the world (evil) and the kingdom (good). While it is true that Scripture talks about the antagonism between the world and the kingdom, it does not condemn our basic creation. The Bible teaches that we often take the good things God has created and misuse them. It is we who can be evil, not the universe. For Catholics, biblical teaching has always maintained that our world is good and has been entrusted to our care by God. We do not see it as something evil to escape; rather we embrace our world without embracing the sin within it.

Bishops of Alabama and Mississippi
(United States), Doc. 44

The fundamentalist approach often leads one to an unbalanced spirituality. Holiness, in this view, comes from fleeing the world: perfect holiness will only be achieved when the world is destroyed.

This gives the lie to the incarnation. Christ Jesus entered the world and began the process of its conversion and transformation. What Adam undid through sin, Christ redoes, and more, through the grace of his redeeming death and resurrection.

Bishops of Alabama and Mississippi
(United States), Doc. 44

As a community we have to understand that the Bible is not a mere answer book for every problem. It is rather the record of God's loving and saving presence among his people. It is his call to us to become a loving, saving presence to one another in the community that is the Church.

Bishops of Alabama and Mississippi
(United States), Doc. 44

The Interpretation of the Bible in the Church

In 1993 the Pontifical Biblical Commission issued the statement The Interpretation of the Bible in the Church, *and although its horizon is broader than the question of the NRMs, some of its comments apply to various fundamentalist groups. It describes this tendency to reject all questioning and to insist on literal meanings as rooted in a rigid ideology that is not biblical. In particular it refuses to "take into account the historical character of biblical revelation" and therefore "historicizes material that from the start never claimed to be historical."*

In its attachment to the principle "Scripture alone," fundamentalism separates the interpretation of the Bible from the Tradition, which, guided by the Spirit, has authentically developed in union with Scripture in the heart of the community of faith. It fails to realize that the New Testament took form within the Christian Church and that it is the Holy Scripture of this Church, the existence of which preceded the composition of the texts. Because of this, fundamentalism is often anti-Church; it considers of little importance the creeds, the doctrines, and liturgical practices that have become part of Church tradition, as well as the teaching function of the Church itself. It presents itself as a form of private interpretation that does not acknowledge that the Church is founded on the Bible and draws its life and inspiration from Scripture.

The fundamentalist approach is dangerous, for it is attractive to people who look to the Bible for ready answers to the problems of life. It can deceive these people, offering them interpretations that are pious but illusory, instead of telling them that the Bible does not necessarily contain an immediate answer to each and every problem. Without saying as much in so many words, fundamentalism actually invites people to a kind of intellectual suicide. It injects into life a false certitude, for it unwittingly confuses the divine substance of the biblical message with what are in fact its human limitations.

Pontifical Biblical Commission, Doc. 22

Discerning the New Age Movement

Much has been written in various parts of the world about the "New Age" movement. It is a product of the syncretist and relativist tendencies that are widespread in today's culture. Like some other NRMs, it diminishes the role of Jesus Christ to one of the many manifestations of the divine in religious history, and is similarly reductive of such central tenets of faith as salvation from sin, the Blessed Trinity, and the role of the Church and its sacraments.

For Christmas 1990 Cardinal Godfried Danneels issued a pastoral letter entitled Christ or Aquarius, *in which he examined the New Age movement. He described it, not as a religion, but as a mixture of science, oriental religiousness, psychology, and astrology—with a special attraction for people in search of some self-fulfilling experience. Among its dangers he diagnosed a cult of the "deep self" that in fact denies the Christian notion of the person, of sin, and of prayer as encounter with God. But where New Age narrows faith into a way of self-experience, the Christian answer lies in the feast of Christmas with its concrete gift of the incarnation of the Son of God.*

The Challenge of New Age to Christianity

New Age is a tremendous challenge to Christianity—not only because it is spreading so vigorously, but primarily because it attacks Christianity directly, while at the same time appropriating whole aspects of the Christian heritage, beginning with the Bible. Moreover, New Age claims to be a new religion, a planetary, universal religion that will take over from all previous religions and bring them all to perfection. New Age is very good at flattering our dreams.

Nevertheless, there are some good things about New Age. It stresses universal brotherhood, peace and harmony, greater awareness, involvement in making the world a better place, general mobilization for good, etc. Moreover, the techniques it promotes are not always bad: yoga and relaxation can have excellent effects.

There is an important distinction to be made: not all that makes us feel good is necessarily good for us, and not all that is pleasurable is necessarily true. This is where the problem lies, for Christians as well as for others.

Cardinal Godfried Danneels, Doc. 56

Positive Aspects of This Trend

It needs to be acknowledged that there are positive features of the New Age movement. It does reflect a commitment to the sacred and spiritual, a rediscovery of the transcendent that is a reaction to the scientific rationalism and the secularism of our day. It seeks truth as the key to all mysteries. It does reflect the seeking in our time of a living, feeling experience of spirituality. It recognizes value in expressing spirituality through signs and symbols, as do the sacraments. It nourishes self-esteem as a necessary ingredient in the search of truth. It is committed to peace, human happiness, good will and benevolence. . . .

Most Rev. Edward Anthony McCarthy, Doc. 46

Distance from the Christian Faith

There is a total omission of a personal God. There is a total omission of God's revelation through Jesus Christ, a total ignoring of the mystery of God's love, of the incarnation, God becoming man in Jesus Christ. There is a total neglect of the redemption through Jesus Christ, of the Holy Spirit, of the Church established by Jesus, of judgment after death, of heaven or hell.

Most Rev. Edward Anthony McCarthy, Doc. 46

Incompatibilities at Three Levels

The question of God: . . . God is not the supreme Lord of a pantheon related to him or deriving from him; he is not the (impersonal) Divine or a nameless transcendental order of all that exists. No, God manifests himself to men as the only God, the only Lord of world and history, in his immutable, personal individuality, as the eternal Other, as the Creator of world and man. But he revealed himself and made known his name, and through his name, he granted to man his saving nearness and presence.

The question of world and man: . . . There is an abyss between God and the world, between God and man: on the one side, there is God, the Creator; on the other, the world and man, a creation. Though the world has come out of the hand of God, making thus visible something divine, this difference has to be taken into account. But precisely because the world is a creation and man a creature of God, it is neither his extension nor his puppet, but something apart and complete in itself.

The question of communication between God or the "divine" and man: Here we discover a decisive difference between Christian faith and *New Age* doctrine: for this last, the world is something divine, and its divine element determines its structure, its law and its evolution; only those who know these divine laws are able to know the heart of the world and to attain, by way of a process of consciousness that leads from ignorance to knowledge, a harmony with the world. The image of man presented by *New Age* is therefore the image of a man who tries to—and even has to—redeem himself. What is important is . . . his supposed capacity to redeem himself, to discover God in himself. . . . Jesus is just one of the masters of spirituality, one of the numerous prophets of the various religions: he is no longer *the Lord.*

Most Rev. Amédée Grab, Doc. 57

The Christ of the New Age

Reference to Christ remains very vague. He is supposed to be a new force, another energy that will one day return in a new form. In fact, for them, the age of Pisces is supposed to have been inaugurated with Christ's coming, that of Aquarius is meant to see the coming of the "new Christ," superior to the former one. In the meantime, it would be necessary to wake up to the spiritual capacity that is in every individual. The concept of the New Age Christ is just this. There is nothing on the life of Jesus; no reference to his death and resurrection. No hint of the Gospel, revelation, the incarnation. According to some theologians, the Christ of the New Age is similar to the Antichrist. He is like Christ, he appears like Christ, but he is opposed to the essence of the Christian faith: Christ, Redeemer of man.

Cardinal Paul Poupard, Doc. 34

A Pseudo-Salvation

Reductions that the New Age has brought to the great concepts of Christianity . . . I summarize in seven points: inner enlightenment replaces the faith that is the obedience of all our being to God; the liberation of one's own creative potential replaces salvation; prayer is transformed into a journey into the depths of the self; a "vague harmony" with the universe substitutes the concrete call to social commitment; theology is overthrown by psychology or theosophy; revelation is found more in the person's heart than in history; and finally, all these reductions-substitutions flow into a vague and ingenuous optimism. This might serve, as they say, to make one "feel better" for a while, but certainly not to give valid responses to tragic problems such as suffering, death, nor even lead to love, true joy, and profound peace.

For us Christians, salvation is liberation from the sin that is in man. Christ alone is the liberator, he who works redemption. . . .

In the New Age there is no need of the Redeemer nor of the cross and resurrection of Christ. Everything is branded with sweetness and sentimentalism, harmony, calm, peace with oneself. Now, we are saved when we are at peace with God, not with ourselves, or rather, each of us will find peace with himself only when he has it with God. If salvation is not understood in this way, we shall end by falling into a sort of selfish well-being, the fruit of an ingenuous optimism.

Cardinal Paul Poupard, Doc. 34

Christian Prayer and Eastern Methods of Meditation

In 1989 the Congregation for the Doctrine of the Faith issued a letter on Some Aspects of Christian Meditation *and warned especially against various dangers involved in attempts to harmonize Christian and oriental techniques of prayer: falling into syncretism, remaining within oneself and not realizing the relationship of creature with Creator, or imagining a dissolving of the personal self into the Absolute.*

The Diversity of Proposals About the Use of Eastern Methods

With the present diffusion of Eastern methods of meditation in the Christian world and in ecclesial communities, we find ourselves faced with a pointed renewal of an attempt, which is not free from dangers and errors, to fuse Christian meditation with that which is non-Christian. Proposals in this direction are numerous and radical to a greater or lesser extent. Some use Eastern methods solely as a psychophysical preparation for a truly Christian contemplation; others go further and, using different techniques, try to generate spiritual experiences similar to those described in the writings of certain Catholic mystics. Still others do not hesitate to place that absolute without image or concepts, which is proper to Buddhist theory, on the same level as the majesty of God revealed in Christ, which towers above finite reality. To this end, they make use of a "negative theology" that transcends every affirmation seeking to express what God is and denies that the things of this world can offer traces of the infinity of God. Thus they propose abandoning not only meditation on the salvific works accomplished in history by the God of the old and new covenant, but also the very idea of the one and triune God, who is love, in favor of an immersion "in the indeterminate abyss of the divinity."

Congregation for the Doctrine of Faith, Doc. 19

The Nature of Christian Prayer

Christian prayer is always determined by the structure of the Christian faith, in which the very truth of God and creature shines forth. For this reason, it is defined, properly speaking, as a personal, intimate and profound dialogue between man and God. It expresses therefore the communion of redeemed creatures with the intimate life of the Persons of the Trinity. This communion, based on baptism and the Eucharist, source and summit of the life of the Church, implies an attitude of conversion, a flight from "self" to the "You" of God. Thus Christian prayer is at the same time always authentically personal and communitarian. It flees from impersonal techniques or from concentrating on oneself, which can create a kind of rut, imprisoning the person praying in a spiritual privatism that is incapable of a free openness to the transcendental God. Within the Church, in the legitimate search for new methods of meditation it must always be born in mind that the essential element of authentic Christian prayer is the meeting of two freedoms, the infinite freedom of God with the finite freedom of man.

Congregation for the Doctrine of Faith, Doc. 19

Humankind as Sharing in the Divine Nature

In order to draw near to that mystery of union with God, which the Greek fathers called the divinization of man, and to grasp accurately the manner in which this is realized, it is necessary in the first place to bear in mind that man is essentially a creature, and remains such for eternity, so that an absorbing of the human self into the divine self is never possible, not even in the highest states of grace. . . .

"God is love" (Jn 4:8). This profoundly Christian affirmation can reconcile perfect union with the otherness existing between lover and loved, with eternal exchange and eternal dialogue. God is himself this eternal exchange, and we can truly become sharers of Christ, as "adoptive sons" who cry out with the Son in the Holy Spirit, "Abba, Father." In this sense, the Fathers are perfectly correct in speaking of the divinization of man, who having been incorporated into Christ, the Son of God by nature, may by his grace share in the divine nature and become a "son in the Son." Receiving the Holy Spirit, the Christian glorifies the Father and really shares in the Trinitarian life of God.

Congregation for the Doctrine of Faith, Doc. 19

Reincarnation or Resurrection?

The word "reincarnation" . . . describes a doctrine that holds that the human soul assumes another body after death. It has, that is, a new incarnation or enfleshment. This is a child of paganism in direct opposition to Scripture and Church tradition, and has been always rejected by Christian faith and theology.

In our time, "reincarnation" has a substantial vogue even in the West, and among many who define themselves as Christians. . . . The reason for its acceptance by many people is possibly due to an instinctive and spontaneous reaction to the rampant materialism of the present day. . . .

[About anthropology:] Christianity defends *duality,* reincarnation defends a *dualism* in which the body is simply an instrument of the soul and is laid aside, existence by successive existence, as an altogether different body is assumed each time. As far as eschatology is concerned, the doctrine of reincarnation denies both the possibility of eternal damnation and the idea of the resurrection of the body. But the fundamental error is in the rejection of the Christian doctrine of salvation. For the reincarnationist the soul is its own savior by its own efforts. Its soteriology is one of auto-redemption, which is diametrically opposed to the heteroredemption of Christian soteriology. In fact, if such a heteroredemption is suppressed, any talk of Christ the Redeemer is null and void. . . . The whole doctrine concerning Church, sacraments and grace stands or falls on this central point.

International Theological Commission, Doc. 18

The response to the doctrine of reincarnation does not consist in condemning other people because of their opinions. But it consists in rediscovering Christian values. The positive truths of Christianity, which offer *the Christian alternative* to the new religiosity's idea of reincarnation are, amongst others, faith in the resurrection of the flesh, of precisely that flesh that we received once and for ever; the Christian understanding of the human body; vigilance as a quality—Jesus demanded it—nourished by the awareness that every moment is irrevocable; the forgiveness of sins, which is immediate and total, even before man has earned it through reconciliation; the dignity of the individual as an image of God, and the absolute rights of the conscience.

Most Rev. Hans Ludvig Martensen, Doc. 58

Authentic Religious Experience

The phenomenon of the new religiosity can present specific characteristics by virtue of its structure to the extent—and in the measure—that it responds to a misleading religious attitude, in which the spirit of the *homo faber* prevails over the spirit of the *homo religiosus*. The authentic religious experience is based on the essence of man as a creature, on the link (*religio*) that man has with a reality that transcends him and in which he is rooted, before which it is necessary first of all to have an attitude of acceptance and gratitude. There is nothing that more deeply contradicts it than the claim to dominate this link, to invent it or to dissolve it. We have seen that some have been able to speak with regard to the new religious movements, of "auto-religion," or to evoke the slightly desecrating but vivid image of the supermarket, the "religious" version of "do-it-yourself." But a "self-religion" becomes, by its very nature and despite appearances, a non-religion.

Most Rev. Giuseppe Casale, Doc. 55

Christian Faith and Human Liberation

The pluralistic nature of society, which seems to be growing everywhere, is a challenge to the Church, perhaps even a factor of renewal. Yet the Church also challenges the new religious movements, offering criteria of discernment between false and true promises. As elements for this discernment the following could be proposed:

- that true faith in the transcendent God safeguards human liberty since it frees from the despotism of other humans;
- that true faith frees from narcissistic tendencies that prevent loving concern for others and service to the community;
- that love and power-seeking do not go together;
- that suffering and death are to be overcome not by evasion but by transfiguring love.

Most Rev. Michael L. Fitzgerald, Doc. 32

Under the oppression of totalitarianism the only people who were able to stay free in heart and belief were those who bound themselves more intensely to God. Faith, adoration and love have a profound relationship with human freedom. Even in "free societies" there are some subtle influences that, like secret seducers, captivate our minds, distort our sensibilities and seek to direct our ways of acting. The person who, in a spirit of adoration of the one true God, bends his knees only to this Lord, is able more easily to reject the multitude of attractive idols.

In fact, the cross and resurrection of Jesus Christ reveal and, through the grace of the Holy Spirit, give that freedom which is worthy of the name. In the history of the life and death of the Lord, it is made clear that the summit of freedom consists in totally free self-giving to the will of the Father for the life of the world. Compared to the full measure of this self-giving, it becomes clear just how much a person can become the servant of self and surrender to powers that enslave him or her.

Synod of Bishops:
Special Assembly for Europe, Doc. 50

"You Shall Not Have Other Gods Before Me"

In the chapter of the Catechism of the Catholic Church *on the first commandment, one finds timely clarifications that help to discern the authentic religious spirit from its counterfeits, such as superstition, idolatry, divination, magic and witchcraft, and spiritism (nos. 2110-2117, Doc. 17). An accurate distinction between religion and magic is made also in the pastoral letter of the bishops of Tuscany entitled* With Regard to Magic and Demonology.

An objective distinction between religion and magic: . . . the distinction derives from the different way with which the two experiences are linked to the transcendent:
• religion means direct reference to God and his action, so much so that there is no religious experience without this reference;
• magic implies a view of the world that believes in the existence of occult powers that influence human life and over which the operator (or the explorer) of magic thinks he is able to exercise control through ritual practices capable of automatically producing effects; recourse to divinity—when there is one—is merely functional, subordinate to these powers and to the desired effects.
Magic does not in fact allow for any superior power above itself; it claims it can oblige the "spirits" or "demons" summoned to manifest themselves and to do what is asked of them. Even today those who have recourse to magic do not first consider referring to God—to the personal God of faith and to his providence in the world—but rather to impersonal occult pow-

ers, superhuman and superterrestrial, reigning over the life of the cosmos and of man. . . .

Magic, in whatever form it is expressed, represents a phenomenon that has nothing to do—on the objective level—with the genuine sense of religion or the cult of God; on the contrary, it is his enemy and antagonist. . . .

Some people . . . have found in magic the expression of a will for power in man, directed to implementing his archetypal dream: to be God. In fact, whatever may be the explanation of motivation, with belief in magic a sort of imitation of that temptation of the ancients is reproduced which was at the root of original sin, present in the heart of man as a tendency, a sly suggestion of the tempter.

Regional Conference of the Bishops of Tuscany
(Italy), Doc. 54

5
PASTORAL CHALLENGES
AND RESPONSES

Many statements from every part of the world emphasize that one of the principal attractions of the new religious movements lies in the vitality of their community life: it involves a dynamism of communication, a sense of belonging, and forms of spontaneous and participative worship.

An equal number of statements list these qualities as constituting challenges to the Catholic Church, as raising questions for self-examination about the relative formality, anonymity, and lack of imagination that can characterize many parish liturgies. The NRMs seek out people where they live and speak to the concerns of their lives: they often use large numbers of lay ministers in their outreach. In some respects the Catholic Church needs to pay attention to the success of these groups in order to stimulate and renew its own language of evangelization.

Among the responses most mentioned are: fostering vitality of faith through small communities; the need to renew the sense of liturgical participation in the Eucharist; the involvement of laypeople in the task of evangelization; a better catechesis in the fundamentals of the faith; the development of a mature sense of the Bible as a source of prayer; the need to respond to particular difficulties of particular NRMs with a differentiated approach, because not every movement is the same.

DOCUMENTS AND DISCOURSES OF POPE JOHN PAUL II

Urgency of This Contemporary Challenge

The sects and the new religious movements today place before the Church a noteworthy pastoral challenge both because of the spiritual and social malaise into which their roots reach, as well as because of the religious elements, which they use as instruments. These elements, taken out of their context in Catholic doctrine and tradition, are often employed for purposes far removed from their original scope.

Message for World Migration Day, Doc. 5

The sects have had great success and their work and influence within the Christian life of your people is significant and can become disastrous. This, then, is one of the most urgent challenges to your pastoral zeal. The urgency of redoubled efforts in evangelization is becoming increasingly evident. Dear brothers, this must involve everyone: priests and laity, especially those with the best training. Your pastoral concern will lead you to take saving action in all areas in which one can discern syncretism that deviates from unity and truth: *"Caritas Christi urget nos."*

To the Bishops of the North-2 Region of Brazil, Doc. 4

If we add to this [the religious relativism] the enterprising proselytism that characterizes some of the especially active and invasive groups, we can immediately see how urgent it is to sustain the faith of believers, giving them the opportunity for a continuous religious formation so that they can always improve their relationship with Christ. This is an extremely great missionary work that God entrusts most of all to you, pastors of his flock, and that requires the commitment of means, a synergy of apostolic initiatives, and most of all, prayer and passionate love for souls.

To Bishops of Abruzzi and Molise (Italy), Doc. 7

Necessity of a New Evangelization

In the magnificent mission of the new evangelization, you must help your communities become increasingly open, welcoming, sensitive to the real conditions of persons who are arriving; seeking to direct them through a real catechesis, either on the level of the Catechetical Pastoral itself, or through directives given during various Eucharistic celebrations or even together with the church movements that give life to many of the dioceses and parishes of your country.

To the Bishops of the North-2 Region of Brazil, Doc. 4

The worrisome phenomenon of the sects must be countered with pastoral action centered on the whole person, on his or her communal dimension and yearning for a personal relationship with God. It is a fact that where the Church's presence is dynamic, such as in parishes where there is a steady formation in the word of God; where the liturgy is active and people participate; where there is a solid Marian piety, true solidarity in the social field, a notable pastoral concern for the family, youth, and the sick, we see that the sects or parareligious movements do not become established or do not make progress.

Because of its eminently Catholic roots, the deep-seated popular religiosity of your faithful, with its extraordinary values of faith and piety, of sacrifice and solidarity, when properly evangelized and joyfully celebrated and directed toward the mysteries of Christ and the Virgin Mary, may serve as antidote to the sects and help safeguard fidelity to the message of salvation.

Opening Address to the IV General Conference of
Latin American Bishops, Doc. 11

Necessity of a Renewed Emphasis on Spirituality

Yet, in the midst of this spiritual confusion, the Church's pastors should be able to detect an authentic thirst for God and for an intimate, personal relationship with him. . . . Pastors must honestly ask whether they have paid sufficient attention to the thirst of the human heart for the true "living water" that only Christ our Redeemer can give (cf. Jn 4:7-13). They should insist on the spiritual dimension of the faith, on the perennial freshness of the Gospel message and its capacity to transform and renew those who accept it.

To the Bishops of Iowa, Kansas, Missouri,
and Nebraska (United States), Doc. 13

Other Documents of the Church

Necessity of a New Evangelization

The Christian message, centered on Jesus Christ who is always alive and present in his Church, must be taught in its entirety, with simplicity and clarity. This proposal is always new, and certainly answers the needs of the human creature, but it always calls for conversion of hearts to the one and true God. This proclamation is to be achieved in all the ways possible; this is a priority in the Church's universal mission, in which the lay faithful have a shared responsibility.

The participants in the consistory therefore insisted on the necessity of promoting a knowledge of sacred Scripture rooted in the Church's tradition and capable of nourishing authentic spirituality and personal prayer. They recalled the importance of welcoming church communities where all people are respected and involved, and where the liturgy and devotions are participative and adapted to the cultural context.

IV Extraordinary Consistory of Cardinals, Doc. 24

Evangelization in the Context of a Syncretistic "New Religiosity"

To evangelize the new religious movements requires three essential things from us:

- that we proclaim the Catholic faith with assurance and clarity, which implies constant deepening and the rediscovery of the rich doctrinal and spiritual heritage of our tradition;
- that we believe and multiply the places where one dares to pray and meditate, speak of mysticism and spirituality; this necessarily means: restoring the fervor, beauty and symbolic dimension of our liturgical celebrations, which can move man's heart; encouraging the vitality of groups, gatherings, and meetings where the fraternal communion of the baptized is lived and expressed;
- that we pay constant attention to the various phenomena characterizing this new religiosity; if we strive to be more familiar with the "sects" and "movements" of which it consists, we will succeed in better understanding their adepts and in undertaking a rich and fruitful dialogue with those of them who are ready for it.

Most Rev. Pierre Raffin, Doc. 59

Sharing Not Only Christian Doctrine, But Religious Experience

The new religious movements promise people wisdom, peace, harmony and self-realization. Our presentation of Christianity should be that of good news, of divine wisdom, of unity and harmony with God and all creation, of happiness that is the earthly preparation for heavenly bliss, and of that peace which the world cannot give (cf. Jn 14:27).

The dimension of religious experience should not be forgotten in our presentation of Christianity. It is not enough to supply people with intellectual information. Christianity is neither a set of doctrines nor an ethical system. It is life in Christ, which can be lived at ever deeper levels.

Cardinal Francis Arinze, Doc. 25

Although our faith includes a "doctrine" and implies "morals" . . .
it is essentially and firstly adherence to Someone who revealed
himself to us; it is a positive response to a proposition of salvation
that God addresses to us in a decisive and irrevocable way in Jesus
Christ; it is a way towards him, a life for him and our brothers, total
abandonment of ourselves to his will, as perfect and faithful an
imitation of his life as possible, an entry into communion with
him who is Love, that is, a gift of himself to the human sinners that
we are. It is a generous and total commitment to witnessing to
Love who revealed himself to us and who urges us to transform
humanity and the world to make it a "civilization of love" (Pope
Paul VI). It has happened, and it still happens, that we so stress the
doctrinal aspect of the moral implication of faith that we forget to
offer our brothers this way of freedom, this way of salvation, this
divine life that is Jesus Christ, the heart, the focal point of the
Good News!

Most Rev. Pierre Raffin, Doc. 59

Evangelizing the Desire for Happiness

In a world in which the variety of choice in the religious field
resembles the shelf of a well-stocked supermarket, how is the quest
for happiness to be evangelized? The Holy Father gives a wonder-
ful example of this in his talks to young people. The VI World
Youth Day in Czestochowa is fresh in the minds of all. The Pope
did not hesitate to present the youth with a high ideal, that of
living as children of God in true freedom. This freedom, he empha-
sized, is both exterior and interior. There is a right to religious
liberty that society must respect. But true freedom includes liberation from sin, the root of all human enslavement. It is a freedom
from evil and for good. Based on respect for the truth about human
nature and creation, it leads to commitment and service.

Most Rev. Michael L. Fitzgerald, Doc. 32

Response to the Quest for a Spiritual Growth

There is a rising interest in spiritual growth among many of our
beloved Catholic people. The emergence of the New Age movement is indeed an indication that the spiritual dimension of life is
being sought by many in our times.

This is both a challenge and an opportunity for the followers of
the Lord. . . . It is a challenge to our clergy, religious and laity to
give a new witness to the spirituality of their faith. It is a challenge
to parish communities to promote spiritual renewal programs, to

become richer centers of prayer, to be more ardent in their liturgical sacramental worship and in many forms of devotion.

It is a time to offer and promote retreats, days of recollection. . . . It is a time to foster many forms of prayer including meditation, contemplation, centering prayer and private devotions. . . . It is time to reflect on the quality of family prayer.

Most Rev. Edward Anthony McCarthy, Doc. 46

A Personal and Integral Approach

People must be helped to know themselves as unique, loved by a personal God, and with a personal history from birth through death to resurrection. *Old truth* should continually become for them *new truth* through a genuine sense of renewal, but with criteria and a framework of thinking that will not be shaken by every *newness* that comes their way. Special attention should be paid to the experiential dimension, i.e., discovering Christ personally through prayer and dedication (e.g., the charismatic and *born again* movements). Many Christians live as if they had never been born at all! Special attention must be given to the healing ministry through prayers, reconciliation, fellowship and care. Our pastoral concern should not be one-dimensional; it should extend, not only to the spiritual, but also to the physical, psychological, social, cultural, economic and political dimensions.

Secretariat for Promoting Christian Unity,
Secretariat for Non-Christians,
Secretariat for Non-Believers,
and Pontifical Council for Culture, Doc. 23

Re-Presentation of a Christian Anthropology

Present a Christian anthropology, which provides the meaning of human potential, the meaning of resurrection, and the meaning of our relationship with the universe. Keep in mind that indifferentism must be combated by adequately presenting the ultimate meaning of the human being.

IV General Conference of Latin American Bishops, Doc. 39

Response to Biblical Fundamentalism

We Catholics have excellent Bible resources and scholars of international repute. Our challenge now is to get this knowledge into the minds, hearts and lives of all our Catholic people. We need a pastoral plan for the word of God that will place the sacred Scriptures at the heart of the parish and individual life. Pastoral creativity can develop approaches such as weekly Bible study groups and yearly Bible schools in every parish. We need to have the introduction to each Bible reading prepared and presented by the lector in a way that shows familiarity with and love for the sacred text. . . . We need to educate—to re-educate—our people knowingly in the Bible so as to counteract the simplicities of biblical fundamentalism.

National Conference of Catholic Bishops
(United States), Doc. 41

1. There is the challenge to read and study, pray over and live the written Word of God.

2. There is the challenge to provide catechesis that will enable Catholics "to make a defense to anyone who calls you to account for the hope that is in you" (1 Pt 3:15), and lead to a mature personal commitment to the Lord Jesus and a living relationship with him, the Father and the Holy Spirit.

3. There is also the challenge to devise pastoral approaches that will reach out to all, especially those who are marginalized in our churches, to make every member of the Church feel that he/she belongs to the Catholic Church in the small communities and parishes

4. There is likewise the challenge to make our liturgies and prayer meetings fraternally warm gatherings of people committed to the Lord. Preparation of biblically based homilies delivered with conviction and the power of the Spirit is seen as an important step towards a more alive liturgical celebration.

5. And finally, there is the challenge to recruit and train lay evangelizers who will confirm their brothers and sisters in the faith through their ministry of the Word of God.

But perhaps the most concrete pastoral strategy adopted by the pastors in the Philippines to counteract the influence of fundamentalist sects is the formation of basic ecclesial communities.

Cardinal Ricardo J. Vidal, Doc. 31

Promotion of Small Ecclesial Communities

There is urgent need for vital participation in small communities. There is great danger in a Church of the masses. The future lies in converting parishes into a community of communities where people feel welcome, where they can experience Christian fraternity, read and reflect together on the Word of God and, by finding through this the strength to live out their lives in a Christian way, to fulfill their evangelizing mission.

Cardinal Angel Suquía Goicoechea, Doc. 29

Today in the United States there is an increasing interest in the formation of such small church communities. Large churches, both Catholic and non-Catholic, are recognizing the potential benefit.

Most Rev. Robert Fortune Sanchez, Doc. 48

Strive to make the Church ever more communitarian and participatory through ecclesial communities, family groups, Bible circles, and ecclesial movements and associations so that the parish becomes a community of communities.

IV General Conference of
Latin American Bishops, Doc. 39

Importance of the Apostolate of the Laity and Especially of the Catechists

Lay ministries are highly effective in counteracting the presence and work of proselytizers. This high visibility of lay ministers/ witnesses has helped transform large city parishes into dynamic loving and serving communities. Each of the ministries becomes a community of its own stressing a particular charism or virtue, affirming one another and sharing a common vision and concern. The Spirit of God works miracles through the instrumentality of these lay ministers.

Most Rev. Robert Fortune Sanchez, Doc. 48

Catechists would seem to be particularly suitable for counteracting the influence of the sects. As they have the task of teaching the faith and of fostering the growth of Christian life, they can help both Christians and non-Christians understand what the real answers to their needs are, without having recourse to the pseudo-securities of the sects. Also, being members of the laity, they are closer to the people and can know their direct and lived situations.

The preferential work-lines for the catechists should be: to study first of all what exactly the sects teach and the points on which they particularly attack the Church, so as to be able to point out the inconsistencies in their position; to forestall their encroachment by giving positive instruction and encouraging the Christian community to greater fervor; and to proclaim clearly the Christian message. They should give personal attention to people and their problems, helping them to clarify doubts and to be wary of the specious promises of the sects.

Congregation for the Evangelization
of Peoples, Doc. 20

Urgency of a Deeper Inculturation of the Gospel in Africa

Several reasons have been put forward for the attractiveness of the sects and independent churches. In these religions people are able to express themselves in celebrations, even to the sharing of their insights into the readings, witnessing and praying as adults in the community. More extensive use is made of the charisms of healing, prophesying, etc., in the community. The Bible is given great prominence and is central in the celebrations. Another reason is the freedom experienced in the sects, freedom in worship, freedom to be oneself, freedom to be at once African and Christian.

Interregional Meeting of Bishops
of Southern Africa, Doc. 37

Need for Greater Attention to the Problems of Healing and Health in Africa

One of the claims of the sects and independent churches is often that of "healing" of both spirit and body, It is here that the Catholic Church is frequently lacking. Priests and other pastoral workers should conduct more services for the sick and for those troubled by "spirits." The Church is seen to be lacking in this care. More such care would offer an alternative to those who would otherwise attend sects for healing services.

Interregional Meeting of Bishops
of Southern Africa, Doc. 37

Other Pastoral Options Underlined by the Latin American Church

Commitment to the poor and marginalized: It is necessary and helpful to insist that it is impossible to believe in Christ and still be indifferent to the problems of our needier brothers and sisters. . . . Therefore we must all be true promoters of justice, peace and reconciliation.

A good family and youth apostolate: In the Latin American world we know the importance of the family; therefore it is necessary to create a good family apostolate so that, beginning with an experience of God and faith in Jesus Christ, the family can assume its true mission of educator in the faith, promotor of development, and adequately form children so that, through a dynamic youth apostolate, they can be true builders of a better world and a civilization based on love.

Popular devotion: This pastoral activity of the Church cannot remain outside our pastoral option in the face of the hounding by the "sects" since it is one of the strongest religious characteristics of our continent; it manifests the inner purity of the faith of our simple people. For the sects it is a point to be attacked; therefore we cannot lay it aside. We must be concerned to give it a greater evangelizing sense and channel the wealth that is found in it.

Use of the mass media: This is a key; if the Church does not use it, we will be very far behind. Therefore the effective use that can be made of the media in evangelization is a great challenge that we must face as a Church that is on pilgrimage in the continent of Latin America.

Cardinal Miguel Obando Bravo, Doc. 28

Need for Adequate Study of and a Pastoral Plan for NRMs

Every diocese or group of dioceses should ask itself searching questions such as the following: What are the sects or new religious movements actually present in its territory? What are their methods of operation? What are the weak points in Catholic life in the area that the NRMs exploit? What practical helps do the lay faithful receive in spirituality and offering of personal prayer? How does the Church in the diocese and its parishes contribute to the building up of genuine support for Christians in material, social or other difficulty? . . . Does the activity of the NRMs in the area indicate that it would be useful if the bishop issued a document for the guidance of the faithful?

Cardinal Francis Arinze, Doc. 25

The Challenge as Potential Blessing

Perhaps we should regard this challenging phenomenon not as a threat, but rather as a catalyst that has succeeded in capturing our attention and thus turned us away from our indifference and false self-satisfaction. It has succeeded in reminding us that we are essentially a missionary church called to spread the good news of God's love and mercy for all people. Active proselytism today will indeed become a blessing for our Catholic Church to the extent that we are able to respond positively and enthusiastically.

Most Rev. Robert Fortune Sanchez, Doc. 48

6
ATTITUDE OF DIALOGUE

What ought to be our attitude towards sects or new religious movements? Is dialogue possible? The inter-dicasterial document of 1986, *Sects or New Religious Movements: Pastoral Challenge,* answered this question in a rather complex manner: one cannot give a general reply, given the diversity of the doctrinal content and of the more or less respectful and sincere attitudes on the part of the NRMs. But certainly our attitude towards the adherents of the NRMs must be inspired by respect for the dignity and the liberty of the human person, by faith in the invisible action of the Spirit, and by the love of Christ towards every person.

John Paul II, after the interreligious meeting at Assisi in October 1986, has stressed the fact that the radical unity of the entire human family, based on a common origin and destiny, is more fundamental than all the differences, even in the religious field (*To the Cardinals and the Roman Curia,* Doc. 1). This positive attitude shows through (as seen in the preceding chapters) when, in reference to the new religiosity, emphasis is given to the value of the spiritual quest of mankind.

In recent documents of the Church, we find texts that underscore the difficulty or impossibility of dialogue when conditions for it are missing, as well as affirmations on the necessity of maintaining towards all the attitude of Christ. Besides, there is a distinction between dialogue at the institutional level (ecumenical, interreligious, cultural, according to the common base that offers a starting point) from the dialogical attitude towards all people, and from the capacity to allow ourselves be challenged by positive values that we can find outside our Church.

Presuppositions for an Ecumenical Dialogue

The Catholic Church is engaged in theological dialogue with eleven other Christian world communions. The basis and justification of these dialogues is the fact that "men who believe in Christ and have been properly baptized are put in some, though imperfect, communion with the Catholic Church" (*Unitatis redintegratio,* no. 3). The Catholic Church recognizes in these churches and ecclesial communities varying degrees of affinity with herself based on the extent to which they share in those gifts that are constitutive of the Church of Christ. This affinity grounds that sense of belonging and of mutual commitment which fuels the ecumenical movement. One of the principal characteristics of a sect is precisely an exclusivity and lack of any sense of belonging to a shared reality: this makes dialogue impossible or at least difficult.

Cardinal Francis Arinze, Doc. 25

Demands of Interreligious Dialogue

Interreligious dialogue demands religious authenticity, purity of intention, an absence of dishonest methods of proselytism. Dialogue with an NRM cannot be ruled out a priori but needs to be preceded by a discernment. This is the meaning of no. 13 of the document Dialogue and Proclamation *published by the Pontifical Council for Interreligious Dialogue together with the Congregation for the Evangelization of Peoples.*

Interreligious dialogue ought to extend to all religions and their followers. This document, however, will not treat of dialogue with the followers of "new religious movements" due to the diversity of situations that these movements present and the need for discernment on the human and religious values each contains.

Congregation for the Evangelization of Peoples and Pontifical Council for Interreligious Dialogue, Doc. 21

Need for a Prior Discernment

This paragraph refers implicitly to the controversies aroused by some movements and is really an invitation to a prudent discernment. A footnote refers to the document of 1986 that goes more fully into the reasons why dialogue with NRMs can be difficult and which counsels against naivety and false irenicism. For some of the movements use methods that run counter to human dignity and freedom, and others are motivated by ideological considerations or economico-political designs that are not in the best interest of humanity.

Most Rev. Michael L. Fitzgerald, Doc. 32

Need for Prudence and Discernment in Relations with Adherents of NRMs

Some people have asked if dialogue with the NRMs is possible. Certainly the nature and the mission of the Church make dialogue with every human being and with religious and cultural groups part of the style of the Church's apostolate. And the Second Vatican

Council has called for dialogue with other Christians and with other believers.

The difficulty lies in how to conduct dialogue with the NRMs with due prudence and discernment. The nature of many NRMs and their manner of operation make dialogue with them particularly problematic for the Church. The duty of pastors of the Church to defend the Catholic faithful from erroneous or dangerous associations is a serious one.

There should be no blanket condemnation of the new religious movements. Catholics should always be ready to study and identify elements or tendencies that are in themselves good or noble and where some collaboration is possible. They should also keep up study and observation of movements that so far present an unclear image.

There remains the problem of the NRMs that pursue an aggressive strategy against the Church, sometimes with foreign economic and political support. Without refusing to discuss with such groups, the Church has to consider how to defend herself with legitimate means.

Cardinal Francis Arinze, Doc. 25

"Double Belonging"

Dialogue comes up against a particular obstacle when we are in contact with movements and groups who, although characterized by precise religious or philosophical doctrines that are different from those of the Catholic faith, ask us for "double membership": in other words, they maintain that it would be perfectly possible to adhere to their movement and to remain in the Catholic Church. This is an ambiguous position, a source of confusion and ultimately harmful to dialogue. Many Eastern religious movements—and some Western—propose "double membership" but teach doctrines such as that of reincarnation, which are absolutely incompatible with the Catholic faith; or propose persons other than Jesus Christ as divine incarnations or messengers of salvation. In all these cases, "double membership" is excluded, and priests must patiently explain to those who have joined these movements that they can no longer consider themselves faithful Catholics nor have recourse to the sacraments.

Great care must also be taken in avoiding any confusion between "double membership" and dialogue. . . . Clarity is necessary because often the episodes and moments of dialogue are exploited by the movements in question, which use them to conclude incorrectly that "double membership" is now permitted.

Most Rev. Giuseppe Casale, Doc. 55

Maintaining the Spirit of Christ in Dialogue

Dialogue with these sects is often difficult because of an unyielding fundamentalism or aggressive proselytizing. Many reject all dialogue outright. With some it may not be locally found prudent to engage in formal dialogue. It is, nevertheless, necessary to develop a Christ-like spirit in relation to all, making the effort to understand them and to enter into dialogue, while recognizing "false prophets" (Mt 24:24), pointing out the inconsistencies in so many of their answers and promises and in some cases warning against the social and political dangers that some sects may pose.

Synod of Bishops: Special Assembly for Africa, Doc. 35

First and foremost, we must start with a principle: even when some Protestants are aggressive towards the Catholic Church, attacking and slandering us, we must recognize, accept and love them like real brothers. We are united to them not only by the fact that as human beings we share in having been created in the image and likeness of God which, basically, is what constitutes human dignity, but also, by the fact that they refer explicitly to Jesus Christ. Even if they conceive of him and accept him only partially, this faith makes our union with them much deeper.

Most Rev. Próspero Penados del Barrio, Doc. 47

Message to Persons Who Have Left the Church to Belong to the NRMs

We ask understanding from those who belong to the groups we have dubbed sects and new religious movements, if we have fallen into errors of expression or interpretation, and if we have not succeeded in making them see all the affection we feel for their persons, created in the image of God, for whom Christ offered his very life. We are also ready to recognize that Jesus can address his comforting words to many of them, whose good faith and sincere way of life we cannot deny: "You are not far from the Kingdom of God" (Mk 12:34).

With equally fraternal honesty, however, we ask them to question themselves, to reflect, to pray, to invoke the enlightenment of the Spirit, to consider their history and to compare it with the thousand-year-old Christian tradition of the people of God, pilgrims on earth who, although they have suffered injuries, schisms and strife, have remained indefectibly faithful to the profession of the faith, to the celebration of the sacraments and to the witness of charity. From this comparison, we dare hope that nostalgia for reconciliation and the unity with the communities they have left who are trustfully awaiting the day of the glorious Lord, will well up in their hearts.

As we await this day, we hope that a frank and fraternal dialogue will be possible which will make us all more vigilant and ready to accept the coming of the Lord (cf. 1 Pt 4:7).

Episcopal Conference of Italy,
Secretariat for Ecumenism and Dialogue, Doc. 52

APPENDIX:
SECTS OR
NEW RELIGIOUS MOVEMENTS:
PASTORAL CHALLENGE

*The Secretariat for Promoting Christian Unity,
the Secretariat for Non-Christians, the Secretariat
for Non-Believers, and the Pontifical Council for Culture.
Vatican, May 3, 1986.*

FOREWORD

In response to the concern expressed by episcopal conferences through-out the world, a study on the presence and activity of sects, new religious movements, and cults has been undertaken by the Vatican Secretariat for Promoting Christian Unity, the Secretariat for Non-Christians, the Secretariat for Non-Believers and the Pontifical Council for Culture. These departments, along with the Secretariat of State, have shared this concern for quite some time.

As a first step in this study project, a questionnaire was sent out in February 1984 to episcopal conferences and similar bodies by the Secretariat for Promoting Christian Unity in the name of the forementioned departments of the Holy See, with the aim of gathering reliable information and indications for pastoral action and exploring further lines of research. To date (October 1985) many replies have been received from episcopal conferences on all continents as well as from regional episcopal bodies. Some replies included detailed information from particular dioceses and were accompanied by copies of pastoral letters, booklets, articles and studies.

NOTE: We publish here the main section of the document, omitting what completes it: the invitation to renewal of the Church from the Extraordinary Synod of Bishops 1985; the list of themes for further study and research; and the bibliography.

It is clearly not possible to summarize the vast documentation received, and which will need to be constantly updated as a basis for a constructive pastoral response to the challenge presented by the sects, new religious movements and groups. The present report can only attempt to give a first overall picture, *and is based on the replies and documentation received.*

---

1. INTRODUCTION

1.1 What Are Sects? What Does One Mean by Cults?

It is important to realize that there exist difficulties in concepts, definitions, and terminology. The terms *sect* and *cult* are somewhat derogatory and seem to imply a rather negative value judgment. One might prefer more neutral terms such as *new religious movements, new religious groups.* The question of the definition of those new movements or groups as distinct from *church* or *legitimate movements within a church* is a contentious matter.

It will help to distinguish sects that find their origin in the Christian religion from those that come from another religious or humanitarian source. The matter becomes quite delicate when these groups are of Christian origin. Nevertheless, it is important to make *this distinction.* Indeed, certain sectarian mentalities and attitudes (i.e., attitudes of intolerance and aggressive proselytism) do not necessarily constitute a sect, nor do they suffice to characterize a sect. One also finds these attitudes in groups of Christian believers within the churches and ecclesial communities. However, those groups can change positively through a deepening of their Christian formation and through the contact with other fellow Christians. In this way they can grow into an increasingly ecclesial mind and attitude.

The criterion for distinguishing between *sects* of Christian origin, on the one hand, and *churches and ecclesial communities,* on the other hand, might be found in the sources of the teaching of these groups. For instance, sects could be those groups that, apart from the Bible, have other *revealed* books or *prophetic messages*; or groups that exclude from the Bible certain proto canonical books, or radically change their content. In answer to question 1 of the questionnaire, one of the replies states:

> For practical reasons a cult or sect is sometimes defined as "any religious group with a distinctive worldview of its own derived

from, but not identical with, the teachings of a major world religion." As we are speaking here of special groups that usually pose a threat to people's freedom and to society in general, cults and sects have also been characterized as possessing a number of distinctive features. These often are that they are authoritarian in structure, that they exercise forms of brainwashing and mind control, that they cultivate group pressure and instill feelings of guilt and fear, etc. The basic work on these characteristic marks was published by an American, Dave Breese, *Know the Marks of Cults* (Victor Books, Wheaton, Ill., 1985).

Whatever the difficulties with regard to distinguishing between sects of Christian origin and churches, ecclesial communities or Christian movements, the responses to the questionnaire reveal at times a serious lack of understanding and knowledge of other Christian churches and ecclesial communities. Some include among sects churches and ecclesial communities that are not in full communion with the Roman Catholic Church. Also adherents of major world religions (Hinduism, Buddhism, etc.) may find themselves classified as belonging to a sect.

1.2 Emergence of New Religious Movements

However, and apart from the difficulties mentioned, almost all the local churches do see the *emergence* and rapid *proliferation* of all kinds of *new* religious or pseudoreligious movements, groups and practices. The phenomenon is considered by almost all the respondents as a *serious matter*, by some as an alarming matter; in only a very few countries there does not seem to exist any problem (e.g., in predominantly Islamic countries).

In some cases the phenomenon appears within the mainline churches themselves (*sectarian attitudes*). In other cases it occurs outside the churches (independent or free churches; messianic or prophetic movements), or against the churches (sects, cults), often establishing for themselves churchlike patterns. However, not all are religious in their real content or ultimate purpose.

1.3 Pastoral Problems

The phenomenon develops fast, and often quite successfully, and poses *pastoral problems*. The most immediate pastoral problem is that of knowing how to deal with a member of a Catholic family who has become involved in a sect. The parish priest or local pastoral worker or adviser usually has to deal first and foremost with the relatives and friends of such a person. Often the person involved can be approached only indirectly. In those cases when the person can be approached directly in order to give him or her guidance, or to advise an ex-member on how to reintegrate into society and the Church, psychological skill and expertise is required.

1.4 The Groups That Are Most Affected

The most *vulnerable* groups in the Church, especially the youth, seem to be the most affected. When they are footloose, unemployed, not active in parish life or voluntary parish work, or come from an unstable family background, or belong to ethnic minority groups, or live in places that are rather far from the Church's reach, etc., they are a more likely target for the new movements and sects. Some sects seem to attract mainly people in the middle-age group. Others thrive on membership from well-to-do and highly educated families. In this context, mention must be made of university campuses that are often favorable breeding grounds for sects or places of recruitment. Moreover, difficult relations with the clergy or an irregular marriage situation can lead one to break with the Church and join a new group.

Very few people seem to join a sect for evil reasons. Perhaps the greatest opportunity of the sects is to attract good people and good motivation in those people. In fact, they usually succeed best when society or Church has failed to touch this good motivation.

1.5 Reasons for Success

The reasons for the success among Catholics are indeed manifold and can be identified on several levels. They are primarily related to the needs and aspirations that are seemingly not being met in the mainline churches. They are also related to the recruitment and training techniques of the sects. They can be external either to the mainline churches or to the new groups: economic advantages, political interest or pressure, mere curiosity, etc.

An assessment of these reasons can be adequately done only from *within the very particular context* in which they emerge. However, the results of a general assessment (and this is what this report is about) can, and in this case do, reveal a whole range of particular reasons that as a matter of fact turn out to be almost universal. A growing interdependence in today's world might provide us with an explanation for this.

The phenomenon seems to be symptomatic of the *depersonalizing structures* of contemporary society, largely produced in the West and widely exported to the rest of the world, which create multiple crisis situations on the individual as well as on the social level. These crisis situations reveal various needs, aspirations, and questions that, in turn, call for psychological and spiritual responses. The sects claim to have, and to give, these responses. They do this on both the affective and the cognitive level, often responding to the affective needs in a way that deadens the cognitive faculties.

These basic needs and aspirations can be described as so many expressions of the human search for wholeness and harmony, participation and realization, on all the levels of human existence and experience; as so many attempts to meet the human quest for truth and meaning, for those constitutive values that at certain times in collective as well as individual history seem to be hidden, broken, or lost, especially in the case of people who are upset by rapid change, acute stress, fear, etc.

1.6 Attitude

The responses to the questionnaire show that the phenomenon is to be seen not so much as a threat to the Church (although many respondents do consider the aggressive proselytism of some sects a major problem), but rather as a pastoral challenge. Some respondents emphasize that, while at all times preserving our own integrity and honesty, we should remember that each religious group has the right to profess its own faith and to live according to its own conscience. They stress that in dealing with individual groups we have the duty to proceed according to the principles of religious dialogue that have been laid down by the Second Vatican Council and in later Church documents. Moreover, it is imperative to remember the respect due to each individual, and that our *attitude* to sincere believers should be one of openness and understanding, not of condemnation.

The responses to the questionnaire show a great need for information, education of believers, and a renewed pastoral approach.

2. REASONS FOR THE SPREAD OF THOSE MOVEMENTS AND GROUPS

Crisis situations or general vulnerability can reveal and/or produce needs and aspirations that become basic motivations for turning to the sects. They appear on the cognitive as well as on the affective level, and are *relational* in character, i.e., centered upon *self* in relation with *others* (social), with the past, present and future (cultural, existential), with the transcendent (religious). These levels and dimensions are *interrelated*. These needs and aspirations can be grouped under nine major headings, although in individual cases, they often overlap. For each group of *aspi-*

rations we indicate what the sects are seen to offer. The main reasons for their success can be seen from that point of view, but one must also take into account the recruitment practices and indoctrinational techniques of many sects (cf. below 2.2).

2.1 Needs and Aspirations; What the Sects Appear to Offer

2.1.1 The Quest for Belonging (Sense of Community)
The fabric of many communities has been destroyed; traditional life styles have been disrupted; homes are broken up; people feel uprooted and lonely. Thus the need to belong.

Terms used in the responses: belonging, love, community, communication, warmth, concern, care, support, friendship, affection, fraternity, help, solidarity, encounter, dialogue, consolation, acceptance, understanding, sharing, closeness, mutuality, togetherness, fellowship, reconciliation, tolerance, roots, security, refuge, protection, safety, shelter, home.

The sects appear to offer: human warmth, care and support in small and close-knit communities; sharing of purpose and fellowship; attention for the individual; protection and security, especially in crisis situations; resocialization of marginalized individuals (for instance, the divorced or immigrants); the sect often does the thinking for the individual.

2.1.2 The Search for Answers
In complex and confused situations, people naturally search for answers and solutions.

The sects appear to offer: simple and ready-made answers to complicated questions and situations; simplified and partial versions of traditional truths and values; a pragmatic theology, a theology of success, a syncretistic theology proposed as *new revelation; new truth,* to people who often have little of the *old* truth; clear-cut directives; a claim to moral superiority; proofs from *supernatural* elements: glossolalia, trance, mediumship, prophecies, possession, etc.

2.1.3 The Search for Wholeness (Holism)
Many people feel that they are out of touch with themselves, with others, with their culture and environment. They experience brokenness. They have been hurt by parents or teachers, by the Church or society. They feel left out. They want a religious view that can harmonize everything and everybody; worship that leaves room for body and soul, for participation, spontaneity, creativity. They want healing, including bodily healing (African respondents particularly insist on this point).

Terms used in the responses: healing, wholeness, integration, integrity, harmony, peace, reconciliation, spontaneity, creativity, participation.

The sects appear to offer: a gratifying religious experience, being saved, conversion; room for feelings and emotions, for spontaneity (e.g., in religious celebrations); bodily and spiritual healing; help with drug or drink problems; relevance to the life situation.

2.1.4 The Search for Cultural Identity

This aspect is very closely linked with the previous one. In many Third World countries, the society finds itself greatly dissociated from the traditional cultural, social and religious values; and traditional believers share this feeling.

The main terms used in the responses are: inculturation/incarnation, alienation, modernization.

The sects appear to offer: plenty of room for traditional cultural/religious heritage, creativity, spontaneity, participation, a style of prayer and preaching closer to the cultural traits and aspirations of the people.

2.1.5 The Need to Be Recognized, to Be Special

People feel a need to rise out of anonymity, to build an identity, to feel that they are in some way special and not just a number or a faceless member of a crowd. Large parishes and congregations, administration-oriented concern and clericalism leave little room for approaching every person individually and in the person's life situation.

Terms used in the responses: self-esteem, affirmation, chances, relevance, participation.

The sects appear to offer: concern for the individual; equal opportunities for ministry and leadership, for participation, for witnessing, for expression; awakening to one's own potential, the chance to be part of an elite group.

2.1.6 The Search for Transcendence

This expresses a deeply spiritual need, a God-inspired motivation to seek something beyond the obvious, the immediate, the familiar, the controllable, and the material, to find an answer to the ultimate questions of life, and to believe in something that can change one's life in a significant way. It reveals a sense of mystery, of the mysterious; a concern about what-is-to-come; an interest in messianism and prophecy. Often the people concerned are either not aware of what the Church can offer, or are put off by what they consider to be a one-sided emphasis on morality or by the institutional aspects of the Church. One respondent speaks of privatized seekers:

Research suggests that a surprisingly large proportion of the population will, if questioned, admit to having had some kind of religious or spiritual experience, say that this has changed their lives in some significant way, and most pertinently add that they have never told anyone about the experience. . . . Many young people say that they have been afraid of being laughed at or thought peculiar were they to broach the subject of spiritual or religious experience and that they have frequently known difficulty in getting teachers or clergy to discuss, let alone answer, their most important and ultimate questions.

Terms used in the responses: transcendence, sacred, mystery, mystical, meditation, celebration, worship, truth, faith, spirituality, meaning, goals, values, symbols, prayer, freedom, awakening, conviction.

The sects appear to offer: the Bible and bible education; a sense of salvation; gifts of the Spirit; meditation; spiritual achievement. Some groups offer not only permission to express and explore ultimate questions in a *safe* social context, but also a language and concepts with which to do so, as well as the presentation of a clear, relatively unambiguous set of answers.

2.1.7 The Need of Spiritual Guidance

There may be a lack of parental support in the seeker's family, or lack of leadership, patience and personal commitment on the part of church leaders or educators.

Terms used: guidance, devotion, commitment, affirmation, leadership, guru.

The sects appear to offer: guidance and orientation through strong, charismatic leadership. The person of the master, leader, guru plays an important role in binding the disciples. At times, there is not only submission, but emotional surrender, and even an almost hysterical devotion to a strong spiritual leader (messiah, prophet, guru).

2.1.8 The Need of Vision

The world of today is an interdependent world of hostility and conflict, violence and fear of destruction. People feel worried about the future; often despairing, helpless, hopeless, and powerless. They look for signs of hope, for a way out. Some have a desire, however vague, to make the world better.

Terms used: vision, awakening, commitment, newness, a new order, a way out, alternatives, goals, hope.

The sects appear to offer: a *new vision* of oneself, of humanity, of history, of the cosmos. They promise the beginning of a new age, a new era.

2.1.9 The Need of Participation and Involvement

This aspect is closely linked with the previous one. Many seekers **not** only feel the need of a vision in the present world society and toward **the** future; they also want to participate in decision making, in planning, **in** realizing.

The main terms used are: participation, active witness, building, **elite,** social involvement.

The sects appear to offer: a concrete mission for a better world, a **call** for total dedication, participation on most levels.

By way of summary one can say that the sects seem to live by what **they** believe, with powerful (often magnetic) conviction, devotion and commitment; going out of their way to meet people where they are, warmly, personally, and directly, pulling the individual out of anonymity, promoting participation, spontaneity, responsibility, commitment . . ., and practicing an intensive follow-up through multiple contacts, home visits, and continuing support and guidance. They help to reinterpret one's experience, to reassess one's values, and to approach ultimate issues in an all-embracing system. They usually make convincing use of the word: preaching, literature, mass media (for Christian groups strong emphasis on the Bible); and often also of the ministry of healing. In one word, they present themselves as the only answer, *the good news* in a chaotic world.

However, although all this mostly accounts for the success of the sects, other reasons also exist, such as the recruitment and training techniques and indoctrination procedures used by certain sects.

2.2 Recruitment and Training Techniques, Indoctrination Procedures

Some recruitment, training techniques, and indoctrination procedures practiced by a number of sects and cults, which often are highly sophisticated, partly account for their success. Those most often attracted by such measures are those who, firstly, do not know that the approach is often staged, and, secondly, are unaware of the nature of the contrived conversion and training methods (the social and psychological manipulation) to which they are subjected. The sects often impose their own norms of thinking, feeling, and behaving. This is in contrast to the Church's approach, which implies full-capacity informed consent.

Young and elderly alike who are at loose ends are easy prey to those techniques and methods that are often a combination of *affection* and *deception* (cf. the *love-bombing*, the *personality test* or the *surrender*). These techniques proceed from a positive approach but gradually achieve a type of mind control through the use of abusive behavior modification techniques.

The following elements are to be listed:

- subtle process of introduction of the convert and his gradual discovery of the real hosts;
- overpowering techniques: love-bombing, offering a free meal at an international center for friends, flirting fishing technique (prostitution as a method of recruitment);
- ready-made answers and decisions are being almost forced upon the recruits;
- flattery;
- distribution of money, medicine;
- requirement of unconditional surrender to the initiator, leader;
- isolation: control of the rational thinking process, elimination of outside information and influence (family, friends, newspapers, magazines, television, radio, medical treatment, etc.) which might break the spell of involvement and the process of absorption of feelings and attitudes and patterns of behavior;
- processing recruits away from their past lives; focusing on past deviant behavior such as drug use, sexual misdeeds; playing upon psychological hang-ups, poor social relationships, etc.;
- consciousness-altering methods leading to cognitive disturbances (intellectual bombardment); use of thought-stopping cliches; closed system of logic; restriction of reflective thinking;
- keeping the recruits constantly busy and never alone; continual exhortation and training in order to arrive at an exalted spiritual status, altered consciousness, automatic submission to directives; stifling resistance and negativity; response to fear in a way that greater fear is often aroused;
- strong focus on the leader; some groups may even downgrade the role of Christ in favor of the founder (in the case of some Christian sects).

3. PASTORAL CHALLENGES AND APPROACHES

A breakdown of traditional social structures, cultural patterns, and traditional sets of values, caused by industrialization, urbanization, migration, rapid development of communication systems, all-rational technocratic systems, etc., leaves many individuals confused, uprooted, insecure, and therefore vulnerable. In these situations there is naturally a search for a solution, and often the simpler the better. There is also the temptation to accept the solution as the only and final answer.

From an analysis of the responses some symptoms of the pathology of many societies today can be listed. Many people suffer from them. They feel anxious about themselves (identity crisis), the future (unemployment, the threat of nuclear war). Questions about the nature of truth and how it is to be found, political uncertainty and helplessness, economic and ideological domination, the meaning of life, oneself and others, events, situations, things, the hereafter.

They suffer a loss of direction, lack of orientation, lack of participation in decision making, lack of real answers to their real questions. They experience fear because of various forms of violence, conflict, hostility; fear of ecological disaster, war and nuclear holocaust; social conflicts, manipulation.

They feel frustrated, rootless, homeless, unprotected; hopeless and helpless and consequently unmotivated; lonely at home, in school, at work, on the campus, in the city; lost in anonymity, isolation, marginalization, alienation, i.e., feeling that they do not belong, that they are misunderstood, betrayed, oppressed, deceived, estranged, irrelevant, not listened to, unaccepted, not taken seriously.

They are disillusioned with technological society, the military, big business, labor, exploitation, educational systems, church laws and practices, government policies.

They might have learned to want to see themselves as conscientious *doers*, not worthless drifters or self-seeking opportunists, but often do not know what to do or how to do it.

They are at a loss at various *in-between* times (between school and university, between school and work, between marriage and divorce, between village and city).

They become empty, indifferent, or aggressive, or they may become *seekers*.

In summary one could say that all these symptoms represent so many forms of alienation (from oneself, from others, from one's roots, culture, etc.). One could say that the needs and aspirations expressed in the responses to the questionnaire are so many forms of a search for *presence* (to oneself, to others, to God). Those who feel lost want to be found. In other words, there is a vacuum crying out to be filled, which is indeed the context in which we can understand not only the criticisms towards the Church that many responses contain, but foremost the pastoral concerns and proposed approaches. The replies to the questionnaire point out many deficiencies and inadequacies in the actual behavior of the Church that can facilitate the success of the sects. However, without further insisting on them, we will mainly emphasize the positive pastoral approaches that are suggested or called for. If these are acted upon, the challenge of the sects may prove to have been a useful stimulus for spiritual and ecclesial renewal.

3.1 Sense of Community

Almost all the responses appeal for a rethinking (at least in many local situations) of the traditional *parish community system;* a search for community patterns that will be more fraternal, more to *the measure of man,* more adapted to people's life situation; more *basic ecclesial communities:* caring communities of lively faith, love (warmth, acceptance, understanding, reconciliation, fellowship), and hope; celebrating communities; praying communities; missionary communities: outgoing and witnessing; communities open to and supporting people who have special problems: the divorced and remarried, the marginalized.

3.2 Formation and Ongoing Formation

The responses put strong emphasis on the need for evangelization, catechesis, education and ongoing education in the faith—biblical, theological, ecumenical—of the faithful, at the level of the local communities, and of the clergy and those involved in formation. (One reply advocates reflective courses for teachers, youth leaders, clergy and religious.) This ongoing process should be both *informative,* with information about our own Catholic tradition (beliefs, practices, spirituality, meditation, contemplation, etc.), about other traditions and about the new religious groups, etc., and *formative,* with guidance in personal and communal faith, a deeper sense of the transcendent, of the eschatological, of religious commitment, of community spirit, etc. The Church should not only be a sign of hope for people, but should also give them the reasons for that hope; it should help to ask questions, as well as to answer them. In this process there is an overall emphasis on the centrality of Holy Scripture. Greater and better use should be made of the mass media of communication.

3.3 Personal and Holistic Approach

People must be helped to know themselves as unique, loved by a personal God, and with a personal history from birth through death to resurrection. *Old truth* should continually become for them *new trust* through a genuine sense of renewal, but with criteria and a framework of thinking that will not be shaken by every *newness* that comes their way. Special attention should be paid to the experiential dimension, i.e., discovering Christ personally through prayer and dedication (e.g., the charismatic and *born again* movements). Many Christians live as if they had never been born at all! Special attention must be given to the healing ministry through prayers, reconciliation, fellowship and care. Our pastoral concern should not be one-dimensional; it should extend, not only to the spiritual, but also to the physical, psychological, social, cultural, economic and political dimensions.

3.4 Cultural Identity

The question of inculturation is a fundamental one. It is particularly stressed by the responses from Africa that reveal a feeling of estrangement to Western forms of worship and ministry, which are often quite irrelevant to people's cultural environment and life situation. One respondent declared:

> Africans want to be Christians. We have given them accommodation, but no home. . . . They want a simpler Christianity, integrated into all aspects of daily life, into the sufferings, joys, work, aspirations, fears and needs of the African. . . . The young recognize in the Independent churches a genuine vein of the African tradition of doing things religious.

3.5 Prayer and Worship

Some suggest a rethinking of the classic Saturday evening/Sunday morning liturgical patterns, which often remain foreign to the daily life situation. The word of God should be rediscovered as an important community-building element. *Reception* should receive as much attention as *conservation*. There should be room for joyful creativity, a belief in Christian inspiration and capacity of *invention* and a greater sense of communal celebration. Here again, inculturation is a must (with due respect for the nature of the liturgy and for the demands of universality).

Many respondents insist on the biblical dimension of *preaching;* on the need to speak the people's language; the need for careful preparation of preaching and liturgy (as far as possible done by a team, including lay participation). Preaching is not mere theorizing, intellectualizing and moralizing but presupposes the witness of the preacher's life. Preaching, worship and community prayer should not necessarily be confined to traditional places of worship.

3.6 Participation and Leadership

Most respondents are aware of the growing shortage of ordained ministers and of religious men and women. This calls for stronger promotion of diversified ministry and the ongoing formation of lay leadership. More attention should perhaps be given to the role that can be played in an approach to the sects—or, at least, to those attracted by the sects—by lay people who, within the Church and in collaboration with their pastors, exercise true leadership, both spiritually and pastorally. Priests should not be identified mainly as administrators, office workers and judges, but rather as brothers, guides, consolers and men of prayer. There is too often a distance that needs to be bridged between the faithful and the bishop, even between the bishop and his priests. The ministry of bishop and priest is a ministry of unity and communion that must become visible to the faithful.

4. Conclusion

In conclusion, what is to be our attitude, our approach to the sects? Clearly, it is not possible to give one simple answer. The sects themselves are too diverse; the situations—religious, cultural, social—too different. The answer will not be the same when we consider the sects in relation to the unchurched, the unbaptized, the unbeliever, and when we are dealing with their impact on baptized Christians, and especially on Catholics or ex-Catholics. Our respondents are naturally concerned mainly with this last group.

Clearly, too, we cannot be naively irenical. We have sufficiently analyzed the action of the sects to see that the attitudes and methods of some of them can be destructive to personalities, disruptive of families and society, and their tenets far removed from the teachings of Christ and his Church. In many countries we suspect, and in some cases know, that powerful ideological forces as well as economic and political interests are at work through the sects that are totally foreign to a genuine concern for the *human* and are using the human for inhumane purposes.

It is necessary to inform the faithful, especially the young, to put them on their guard, and even to enlist professional help for counseling, legal protection, etc. At times we may have to recognize, and even support, appropriate measures on the part of the state acting in its own sphere.

We may know, too, from experience that there is generally little or no possibility of dialogue with the sects; and that not only are they themselves closed to dialogue, but they can also be a serious obstacle to ecumenical education and effort wherever they are active.

And yet, if we are to be true to our own beliefs and principles: respect for the human person, respect for religious freedom, faith in the action of the Spirit working in unfathomable ways for the accomplishment of God's loving will for all humankind, for each individual man, woman and child, we cannot simply be satisfied with condemning and combating the sects, with seeing them perhaps outlawed or expelled, and individuals *deprogrammed* against their will. The *challenge* of the new religious movements is to stimulate our own renewal for a greater pastoral efficacy.

It is surely also to develop within ourselves, and in our communities, the mind of Christ in their regard; trying to understand *where they are*, and, where possible, reaching out to them in Christian love.

We have to pursue these goals, being faithful to the true teaching of Christ, with love for all men and women. We must not allow any preoccupation with the sects to diminish our zeal for true ecumenism among all Christians.